OSPREY AIRCRAFT OF THE

Croatian Aces
of World War 2

SERIES EDITOR: TONY HOLMES

OSPREY AIRCRAFT OF THE ACES® • 49

Croatian Aces of World War 2

Dragan Savic & Boris Ciglic

OSPREY
PUBLISHING

Front cover
Around midday on 23 April 1945, the commanding officer of 2. *Lovacko Jato* **ZNDH, satnik Ljudevit Bencetic (flying Bf 109G-10 'Black 22'), together with his wingman, porucnik Mihajlo Jelak (in Bf 109G-14 'Black 27'), were returning to Lucko airfield after an uneventful patrol when, east of Zagreb, they spotted two RAF Mustang IVs of No 213 Sqn below them. Although Croat pilots generally avoided combat with Allied aircraft at this late stage of the war, this was an opportunity too good to be missed. They approached undetected and attacked, Bencetic firing from a distance of 260 ft (80 m). Hitting the Mustang's radiator and wings, he succeeded in setting the RAF fighter on fire. Flg Off F J Barrett, flying Mustang Mk IVA KH869, tried to escape, but Bencetic's second burst from an even shorter distance tore into his aircraft's fuselage and forced him to crash-land in the Turopolje area, where friendly Partisans saved him from capture.**

In the meantime, Jelak had attacked the second British fighter, and he claimed to have shot it down when two more Mustangs appeared and heavily damaged his aircraft, forcing him to crash-land near Velika Gorica, close to the Zagreb–Sisak railway line. In reality, there were four No 213 Sqn aircraft in the area, but only one pair became involved with the Croats, and Jelak was actually a victim of the pilot he was thought to have shot down, Flt Lt Graham Hulse, who was flying Mustang Mk IVA KH826. Hulse duly claimed a Bf 109 damaged in the Okucani–Zagreb area. The whole combat lasted some ten minutes at different heights, starting at 6,500 ft (2,000 m) and descending down to treetop height. Bencetic's 16th confirmed kill was also the last aerial victory achieved by a Croatian pilot in World War 2 (*cover artwork by Iain Wyllie*)

First published in Great Britain in 2002 by Osprey Publishing
Elms Court, Chapel Way, Botley, Oxford, OX2 9LP

© 2002 Osprey Publishing Limited

ISBN 1 84176 435 3

Edited by Tony Holmes and Bruce Hales-Dutton
Page design by Tony Truscott
Cover Artwork by Iain Wyllie
Aircraft Profiles by John Weal
Scale Drawings by Mark Styling
Origination by Grasmere Digital Imaging, Leeds, UK
Printed in China through Bookbuilders

EDITOR'S NOTE
To make this best-selling series as authoritative as possible, the Editor would be interested in hearing from any individual who may have relevant photographs, documentation or first-hand experiences relating to the world's elite pilots, and their aircraft, of the various theatres of war. Any material used will be credited to its original source. Please write to Tony Holmes at 10 Prospect Road, Sevenoaks, Kent, TN13 3UA, Great Britain, or by e-mail at: tony.holmes@osprey-jets.freeserve.co.uk

ACKNOWLEDGEMENTS
The publication of this book would not have be possible without the generous help of the following ex-VVKJ, ZNDH and JRV airmen, and their families:

Ljudevit Aladrovic, Zdenko Avdic, Ivan Baltic, the family of Eduard Banfic, the family of Bozidar Bartulovic, Andrija Blazevic, Josip Bolanca, Vladimir Bosner, the family of Safet Boskic, the family of Ivan Cvencek, Nikola Cvikic, the family of Janko Dobnikar, Sime Fabijanovic, Vladimir Ferencina, the family of Grigorije Fomagin, Nikola Kaledin, Stanko Forkapic, Desimir Furtinovic, Franc Godec, the family of Djuro Gredicak, Josip Helebrant, the family of Mihajlo Jelak, Tomislav Kauzlaric, Marijan Kokot, the family of Asim Korhut, Boris Koscak, Nenad Kovacevic, Vladimir Kres, the family of Ivan Kulic, Ignacije Lucin, Martin Mak, Ivan Masnec, Mladen Milovcevic, Roko Mirosevic, the family of Nikola Obuljen, Djuro Perak, Josip Persic, the family of Milan Persic, Jakob Petrovic, the family of Misko Pintaric, Zvonko Planinc, Tugomir Prebeg, the family of Ivan Pupis, Luka Puric, Josip Rupcic, Josip Santovac, Tihomir Simcic, Ernest Somer, Albin Starc, Stjepan Starjacki, Daut Secerbegovic, Alojz Seruga, the family of Krunoslav Skeva, Kresimir Sneler, the family of Vladimir Spoljar, Djuro Svarc, Bogdan Vujicic, Vladimir Zagajski (Ahmetagic) and Dragutin Zauhar.

CONTENTS

PROLOGUE

The creation of Yugoslavia in 1918 was, historians said, a shotgun wedding. Indeed, the Kingdom of Serbs, Croats and Slovenes was often an uneasy and at times turbulent place almost from the moment of its formation.

Besides Serbia, Croatia and Slovenia, the Kingdom was also comprised of Bosnia-Herzegovina, Montenegro and Macedonia, together with two large autonomous Serbian provinces, Vodjvina and Kosovo. This disparate collection of nationalities, cultures and creeds, which for good measure also included Hungarians, Germans and Albanians, co-existed in the shadow of the often tense relationship between the two largest ethnic groups, the Serbs and the Croats.

Although there are no obvious racial differences between them, the divisions between Serbs and Croats have dominated the region's history. The Serbs had thrown off the Ottoman yoke in the 19th century, while the Croats had been associated with the Austro-Hungarian Habsburg Empire until 1918. And although Serbs and Croats speak virtually the same language, the Serbs use the Cyrillic alphabet and the Croats the Latin. Finally, the Serbs predominantly worship in the Orthodox Church, whilst the Croats are mainly Catholics.

Between the two world wars, these differences were exacerbated by a weak economy and by the territorial claims of neighbouring states – particularly Italy – which had designs on parts of Slovenia and Croatia. Tensions reached a peak after the Croat leader Stjepan Radic and other deputies were gunned down in parliament in June 1928 by a Montenegrin assassin, at Italy's instigation, as has recently been established.

To stabilise the situation, King Alexander dissolved Parliament in January 1929 and imposed a centralised and repressive dictatorship. Some of the more radical Croats emigrated, and one of them, Ante Pavelic, with the support of Italy and Hungary, formed the *Ustasa* terrorist organisation, which sought the creation of an independent Croat state.

In 1934, while on a state visit to France, the King was assassinated in Marseille. Although the perpetrators were Macedonian nationalists and *Ustasa* gunmen, it was not difficult to discern the hand of Mussolini behind the murder. A final, but ultimately unsuccessful, attempt to pull the country together came with the 1939 Serb-Croat agreement, which set up an autonomous province, or *Banovina*, under which Croatia would be governed by a crown appointee or *ban*.

Yugoslav foreign policy had previously been aligned towards France, but under Prince Paul, Alexander's Oxford-educated cousin who became regent on the King's death, it shifted towards Germany. In the early 1930s a series of trade agreements with Berlin helped pull Yugoslavia out of the depression.

Franco-British appeasement of German ambitions also pushed the country reluctantly towards the Axis camp. Yet when World War 2 started in September 1939, Yugoslavia attempted to remain neutral. However, the pressure mounted with Italy's botched attack on Greece, which increased Hitler's determination to deny the British a foothold in southern Europe. On 25 March 1941 Yugoslavia signed a treaty with the Axis powers.

Days later a group of officers, encouraged by the British Special Operations Executive, staged a *coup d'etat*, proclaimed Alexander's 17-year-old son Peter as King and denounced the treaty. Inevitably, this action was welcomed in London and Washington, Churchill declaring that Yugoslavia had found its soul. The body, though, was about to provide a feast for the country's covetous neighbours, for Hitler's response would be both swift and typically brutal.

GLOSSARY

VVKJ – *Vazduhoplovstvo Vojske Kraljevine Jugoslavije* (Royal Yugoslav Air Force)
PV – *Pomorsko Vazduhoplovstvo* (Naval Air Force)
VP – *Vazduhoplovni Puk* (Aviation Regiment)
BE – *Bombarderska Eskadrila* (Bomber Squadron)
BG – *Bombarderska Grupa* (Bomber Group)
BP – *Bombarderska Puk* (Bomber Regiment)
LE – *Lovacka Eskadrila* (Fighter Squadron)
LG – *Lovacka Grupa* (Fighter Group)
LP – *Lovacka Puk* (Fighter Regiment)
PS – *Pilotska Skola* (Pilot School)

HZIS – *Hrvatska Zrakoplovna Izobrazbena Skupina* (Croatian Air Force Training Group)
DPJ – *Docastnicko Popunidbeno Jato* (Non-commissioned Officers' Training Squadron)
LJ – *Lovacko Jato* (Fighter Squadron)
LS – *Lovacka Skupina* (Fighter Group)
ZJ – *Zrakoplovno Jato* (Air Force Squadron)
ZLJ – *Zrakoplovno Lovacko Jato* (Air Force Fighter Squadron)
ZLS – *Zrakoplovno Lovacka Skupina* (Air Force Fighter Group)

NDH – *Nezavisna Drœava Hrvatska* (Independent State of Croatia)
ZNDH – *Zrakoplovstvo Nezavisne Drzave Hrvatske* (Air Force of Independent State of Croatia)
HZL – *Hrvatska Zrakoplovna Legija* (Croatian Air Force Legion)
HZS – *Hrvatska Zrakoplovna Skupina* (Croatian Air Force Group)

NOP – *Narodnooslobodilacki Pokret* (People's Liberation Movement)
NOVJ – *Narodnooslobodilacki Vojska Jugoslavije* (People's Liberation Army of Yugoslavia)
JA – *Jugoslovenska Armija* (Yugoslav Army)
JRV – *Jugoslovensko Ratno Vazduhoplovstvo* (Yugoslav Air Force)
LD – *Lovacka Divizija* (Fighter Division)

Royal Yugoslav Air Force Order of Battle on 6 April 1941*

1. Aviation Fighter Brigade:
Belgrade — 1 Messerschmitt Bf 109E-3a
2. Fighter Regiment:
Kragujevac and Kraljevo — 15 Hurricane Is
19 Messerschmitt Bf 109E-3as

6. Fighter Regiment:
Zemun and Krusedol — 6 Rogozarski IK 3s,
32 Messerschmitt Bf 109E-3as
2 Potez Po 63s

7

2. Combined Aviation Brigade:
Nova Topola
4. Fighter Regiment:
Bosanski Aleksandrovac   8 Ikarus IK-2s
                                           20 Hurricane Is

8. Bomber Regiment:
Rovine   24 Blenheim Is

3. Combined Aviation Brigade:
Stubol
3. Bomber Regiment:
Petrovac and Stubol   60 Dornier Do 17Ks
5. Fighter Regiment:
Rezanovacka Kosa and Kosancic   25 Hawker Fury IIs
                                           1 Avia BH-33E

4. Aviation Bomber Brigade:
Ljubic
1. Bomber Regiment:
Bijeljina and Davidovac   24 Blenheim Is
7. Bomber Regiment:
Preljina and Gorobilje   26 Savoia Marchetti SM.79s

Units under direct VVKJ Staff command
11. Independent Aviation Group for long reconnaissance:
Veliki Radinci   9 Blenheim Is
                                           2 Hawker Hind Is
81. Independent Aviation Bomber Group:
Ortijes   14 Savoia Marchetti SM.79s

Auxiliary Air Force
III Pilot School:
Mostar   2 Avia BH-33Es**
                                           2 Messerschmitt Bf 109E-3as
                                           3 Hurricane Is

Bomber School:
Mostar   3 Dornier Do 17Ks
Test Group:
Kraljevo   1 Messerschmitt Bf 110C-4,
                                           1 LVT-1***
603. Training Squadron   1 Rogozarski R 313

Notes
* The VVKJ received eight additional Hurricane Is, six Do 17Ks, four Blenheim Is, two IK 2s, 1 Bf 109E-3a and one IK 3 between 6 and 17 April 1941. Other miscellaneous army and PV (naval air force) units mustered around 530 obsolete aircraft of various types, as well as about 75 water-borne machines.

** there were five Avia BH-33Es, but three were unarmed and the remaining two had only one machine gun each.

*** Hurricane I with a Daimler-Benz DB 601 engine.

DEATH OF AN AIR FORCE

Realising that war in Europe was inevitable, the *Vazduhoplovstvo Vojske Kraljevine Jugoslavije* (VVKJ – Royal Yugoslav Air Force) embarked upon an ambitious modernisation programme during the late 1930s. Plans were made to buy and produce modern aircraft, and for an expanded aircrew training programme. Under the circumstances this proved to be unrealistic, and the VVKJ went to war with just 102 modern fighters, 151 bombers and nine operational reconnaissance aircraft (see order of battle in the Prologue) to oppose the 797 fighters, 965 bombers and 339 reconnaissance machines deployed by the Luftwaffe, Italy's *Regia Aeronautica* and the Hungarian air force.

Yet although Yugoslav aircrew lacked experience of modern air fighting, and were deficient in formation flying, 'blind' flying and tactical knowledge, their morale remained high.

During March 1941 the VVKJ was clandestinely mobilising so that when the Germans invaded, the vast majority of its aircraft had been dispersed to about 50 auxiliary airfields. Although mostly well executed, this mobilisation was to lead to difficulties during operations, especially for fighter units, because the air force command had failed to organise an adequate support structure to bring together the dispersed units when they were most needed – in the air.

Franjo Dzal, who was one of the best-known pre-war VVKJ pilots, and the future head of the HZL, prepares to taxi out in Dewoitine D.1 C1 'No 13' during the early 1930s (*A Ognjevic*)

To make matters worse, on 3 April kapetan I klase Vladimir Kren, a future Commander in Chief of the *Zrakoplovstvo Nezavisne Drzave Hrvatske* (ZNDH – air force of the Independent State of Croatia), defected to Austria in a Potez Po 25, taking with him much valuable intelligence about the VVKJ.

At dawn on 6 April 1941, the German invasion of Yugoslavia began. The first air-attacks were launched from bases in Bulgaria by units of *VIII Fliegerkorps*, which struck targets in southern Serbia and Macedonia. These attacks were swiftly followed up by units of *Luftflotte 4*, stationed in Austria, Hungary and Rumania. Their objective was Belgrade, and its surrounding airfields. Finally, units of *X Fliegerkorps* and the Italian *Comando Aeronautica Albania* 2a and 4a *Squadra Aerea* were assigned targets along the Adriatic coast, including Podgorica, Mostar and Sarajevo.

The main ground thrusts came from two directions. In the south, one element of the *Wehrmacht's* 12. *Armee* attacked from Bulgaria. Splitting into three, it pushed the defenders back and quickly advanced to Skoplje, Strumica and Bitolj. By 10 April it had occupied most of Macedonia. The rest of 12. *Armee* struck north towards Belgrade, capturing Nis on the 9th. In the north, units of 2. *Armee* attacked from Austria and Hungary. They quickly overran Slovenia and entered Zagreb on the 10th, continuing on to Sarajevo, which fell five days later. A second column from Hungary drove towards Belgrade, and the ruined city fell on the 13th. Italian and Hungarian troops also took part in these actions, although they only played a minor role.

The defenders fought bravely, but they faced an enemy with both numerical and material superiority. Defeat was hastened by bad co-ordination, lack of initiative by some senior commanders and, on occasion, betrayal. After senior government figures fled the country, the Yugoslav Army capitulated on 17 April.

In general, the VVKJ and the PV had fought well, but had suffered heavy losses – 142 airmen (including about a dozen Croats) were killed. Around 50 VVKJ fighters were lost, resulting in the death of 22 pilots. In return, they claimed more than 50 enemy aircraft destroyed, although they actually inflicted losses of about 35.

Pilots of 6.LP and III PS come together at Zemun airfield for a group photograph in front of a Hawker (Yugoslav) Hind I during the late 1930s. In the centre of the shot, wearing a full-length leather coat, is Russian pilot maj Vladimir Tihomirov, and to his left is maj Franjo Dzal. At the outbreak of war Dzal was deputy CO of 5.LP. In the early morning of 6 April 1941, as a formation of some 40 Luftwaffe Bf 109s and Bf 110s attacked Rzanovacka Kosa airfield, he avoided take-off and watched from the ground as his men from 36.LG were slaughtered in their obsolete biplane fighters. In an unequal battle against superior adversaries, ten Furies – five of them still in the process of taking off – were shot down and eight VVKJ pilots killed. Two more Furies, a Jungmann and an RWD 13 were also destroyed on the ground. In return, the Yugoslav pilots shot down three Bf 109s and a Bf 110, and damaged a handful of aircraft from I.(J)/LG 2, II.(Sch)/LG 2 and II./ZG 26 (*A Ognjevic*)

A Dornier Do 17K of 205.BE sits on the ground at Petrovac airfield in the summer of 1940. Altogether, 36 Do 17Ks were delivered to the VVKJ from Germany, with a further 36 examples being built under licence at DFA, in Kraljevo. A number of Croatian fighter pilots who saw action on the Russian front had flown the Do 17 pre-war (*P Bosnic*)

The Bf 109E-3a was the most potent fighter in the VVKJ inventory at the outbreak of war, but pilots with as little as 50 flying hours on the type were considered 'experienced', especially as the average was around 25 hours. 'L-2', 'L-83' and 'L-13' of III PS were photographed at Nis airfield on 9 August 1940. The very next day the unit's CO, maj Vladimir Tihomirov, wrecked 'L-83' when he forgot to extend its landing gear (*M Micevski*)

Many of the surviving Croat pilots took a less than dim view of the German occupation. Indeed, some *Ustasa* supporters were openly pro-German, refusing to fight and betraying their country and their fellow airmen. For example, the CO of 3. *Bombarderski Puk* (BP – bomber regiment) refused to move his unit's Do 17s to an auxiliary airfield, and instead left them unprotected at Petrovac, near Skoplje.

Soon spotted by the Germans on 6 April, the bombers were attacked by four Ju 87s and 17 Bf 109s at dawn. Of the 30 63. *Bombarderska Grupa* (BG – bomber group) Do 17s at the airfield, 16 were destroyed and 10 damaged. The four remaining Dorniers were sent to Urosevac airfield, although one stalled on take-off and crashed, killing a crew member and seriously wounding both the pilot, narednik-djak Nikola Vice, and his gunner. A second attack that afternoon destroyed the remaining aircraft.

On 7 April, according to one report, maj Mato Culinovic, CO of 205. *Bombarderska Eskadrila* (BE – bomber squadron)/63.BG/3.BP, ignored orders to withdraw to Greece and instead dismissed his men and told them to go home. A few days later he was seen in Skoplje having a friendly chat with German officers.

In Zemun, pukovnik Dragutin Rubcic, CO of 1. *Lovacka Brigada* (LB – fighter brigade) dismissed major Adum Romeo, CO of 51. *Lovacka Grupa* (LG – fighter group), for 'rejection of orders and open cowardice'.

Some Croats, on the other hand, fought vigorously. Narednik-vodnik I klase Tomislav Kauzlaric of 104. *Lovacka Eskadrila* (LE – fighter squadron)/32. LG/6. *Lovacka Puk* (LP – fighter regiment) was ready in his Bf 109E-3a at Krusedol auxiliary airfield when the first wave of German bombers attacked Belgrade on 6 April. Indeed, he and his element leader, Serbian maj Danilo 'Daca' Djordjevic, CO of 32.LG, were the last to leave Krussedol at 0730 hrs;

'We saw a lone Messerschmitt Bf 110. Daca commenced an attack from above and at 300 m distance. He missed and overshot, and the gunner fired back. He then turned for a head-on attack, but when the

Por Vilim Acinger poses in front of a Hawker (Yugoslav) Fury II in August 1940. As a member of 104.LE, Acinger flew three sorties during the April war but failed to score any kills. Of German descent, he later joined the ZNDH and HZL. Although some sources credit him with nine and others as many as 16 kills, he actually claimed a single victory before returning to Croatia due to illness in the spring of 1942. He was executed by JA forces following his capture in Slovenia in May 1945 (*M Micevski*)

III PS Instructors kap Ik Zlatko Stipcic (extreme left) and nv IIIk Milan Delic (extreme right) pose with groundcrewmen at Nis in 1940. Having amassed 250 flying hours on *Emils*, Stipcic was one of the most experienced VVKJ pilots on the type. A Croatian Serb, Delic defected from the ZNDH to Turkey with his crew in a Bristol Blenheim on 9 July 1942. He later flew 48 sorties with the RAF's Spitfire V-equipped No 352 (Yugoslav) Sqn (*M Hrelja*)

German fired he broke hard downwards. At that moment I approached at high speed from behind and underneath and fired my cannon into his belly. The Bf 110 exploded [author's note – this was one of two 2./ZG 26 aircraft lost in that area, both pilots, Leutnant Reinhold Eymers and Oberfeldwebel Willi Messemer, and their gunners, being killed], and I flew through its debris and fire. I broke hard to port and saw it crash near our airfield.

'I turned in the direction of Belgrade and saw a group of Heinkel He 111s (actually Ju 88s from KG 51). I attacked from the side. I could see tracer coming in my direction as all the bombers fired at me. I attacked one that was out of formation, but it escaped into cloud. I think I hit him. I heard later that it fell in Backa, but it was never confirmed.'

This sortie would prove to be Kauzlaric's only mission in the April war because, as he said, 'there were too many volunteers and too few aircraft'. The very next day another pilot lost his life in the aircraft Kauzlaric had flown that morning.

Kapetan II klase Bozidar Ercigoj and narednik II klase Zvonimir Halambek, also from 104.LE, took off from Krusedol minutes before Kauzlaric on 6 April. Soon, they were attacking a formation of '30 Do 17s' (actually Bf 110s), and Halambek claimed one – probably the second aircraft lost by 2./ZG 26. He observed it falling in flames, but another Bf 110 damaged his *Emil* and he belly-landed near Krusedol.

The next day, at 1420 hrs (some sources state it was on 6 April), Halambek and Slovene narednik I klase Veljko Stalcer chased a high-flying reconnaissance aircraft. They lost it in cloud, but encountered Ju 88s of KG 51 returning from a mission to Belgarde. Halambek attacked one and later, in captivity, the bomber's gunner said that the Croat's fire had killed the pilot and navigator. After four more Yugoslav pilots attacked it, the Junkers bomber crashed near the village of Kac. Groundcrew from Krusedol rushed to the scene to collect usable 7.9 mm ammunition, which they desperately needed to arm their own aircraft.

On the morning of the 8th, Halambek, on his sixth operational mission, piloted one of the remaining fighters from Krusedol to Radinci airfield. He later fled to Greece in a Caproni Ca.310 following the fall of Yugoslavia. Halambek would eventually die on 1 July 1944 when his RAF Spitfire Mk V (JG920) was involved in a flying accident in Libya whilst he was serving with No 352 (Yugoslav) Sqn.

Also active in the tense days of April 1941 was kapetan I klase Zlatko Stipcic of III *Pilotska Skola* (PS – Pilot School), stationed near Mostar. On his second sortie on 6 April, at 1130 hrs, he damaged one of ten Cant Z.1007s of 47° *Stormo BT* that were attacking Mostar. Later, he claimed a Ju 88 over the Adriatic near the Peljesac peninsula, this aircraft probably being 8./LG 1's Ju 88A-5 Wk-Nr 2269, which was written off after a crash-landing at Grottaglie airfield, in Italy, after

suffering 'engine trouble'. Leutnant Erwin Pruckner and two crew members were wounded.

On his return to Kosor, Stipcic was attacked by a Bf 110, his aircraft suffering slight damage. Nevertheless, his attacker, Oberfeldwebel Richard Heller of III./ZG 26, claimed the Croat as his fifth of an eventual 22 victories.

One of Stipcic's pupils in III PS was porucnik Ivan Rubcic, who claimed a Z.1007 on 8 April over the Neretva estuary while flying a Hurricane.

After the Independent State of Croatia was proclaimed on 10 April, narednik vodnik III klase Cvitan Galic, a pre war *Ustasa* member and a man who was to make a name for himself on the Eastern Front, landed a Bücker Jungmann at an airfield occupied by Croat rebels. Provisional Croat markings were applied to the aircraft and Galic, previously an instructor at III PS, made a few reconnaissance flights in the diminutive biplane.

When Yugoslav resistance finally crumbled, the Croat pilots went their separate ways. Some evaded capture and returned to their homes, others escaped to the Soviet Union and the Middle East to continue the fight on the allied side, and a significant number were rounded up and sent to prisoner of war camps for the next four years. Most, however, joined the newly formed Croatian air arm. All, though, faced an uncertain future.

The VVKJ entered the war with 38 Hurricanes Is, some of which were Hawker-manufactured and others built under licence at the Zmaj factory. Hurricane pilots gained at least six confirmed and four probable victories, although six were killed and four injured in the process. This photograph shows Hurricanes lined up at Zemun airfield on 27 April 1940, awaiting an inspection by King Peter (*S Ostric*)

nv IIIk Cvitan Galic and k Ik Miho Klavora converse in front of Bf 109E-3a 'L-65' during manoeuvres at Veliki Radinci in September 1940. A Slovene, and deputy CO of 103.LE, Klavora was killed during combat with Luftwaffe Bf 109s (probably from JG 77) on 7 April 1941. Eyewitnesses on the ground – among them Tomislav Kauzlaric – stated that he shot down two Bf 109s moments before crashing to his death near Krusedol monastery (*S Ostric*)

THE EASTERN FRONT

W hen, on 10 April 1941, troops of the 14th *Panzer* division entered the Croatian capital, Zagreb, they expected to be received as conquerors. Instead, they were hailed as liberators from Serbian oppression.

As the Yugoslav campaign had not been on his immediate agenda, Hitler had formulated no plans for the country's occupation. Nor had he been sure of the reception he would receive in the Balkans. In the event, the *Führer* decided to hive off whatever he could to neighbouring countries with territorial claims. As a result, Slovenia was divided between Germany, Italy and Hungary. Italy, which already possessed Istria, also grabbed much of Dalmatia and established a Montenegrin protectorate. Some areas of Croatia went to Hungary, while Bulgaria acquired Macedonia, as well as parts of Serbia. Albania, already an Italian protectorate, absorbed Kosovo. Most of Serbia, parts of Croatia and Bosnia-Herzegovina became a German protectorate, but control over what remained of Croatia – most of the former *Banovina*, the remainder of Bosnia-Herzegovina and Srem, with a total population of 6.3 million – was handed over to Ante Pavelic and the *Ustasa*.

On the day the Germans entered Zagreb, the Independent State of Croatia (NDH – *Nezavisna Drœava Hrvatska*) came into existence. The formation of the Croatian Army was announced on 19 April, seven days after Slavko Kvaternik took command of 'all military powers of the Croatian State', while the newly promoted pukovnik Vladimir Kren headed all air forces 'because of his special merits, and long years of work for the *Ustasa* movement'.

On 27 June the Croatian Legion (*Hrvatska Legija*) was formed on Pavelic's orders to mark the new state's gratitude to Hitler. Its creation followed just days after the Wehrmacht's invasion of the Soviet Union, and the legion's purpose was to fight alongside Germans on the Eastern Front. It would comprise infantry, naval and aviation units, with the air component, *Hrvatska Zrakoplovna Legija* (HZL – Croatian Air Force Legion) being established on 12 July. Named 4. *Mesovita Zrakoplovna Pukovnija* (Mixed Air Force Regiment), and commanded by Oberstleutnant

Major Dzal (left) and an unknown Luftwaffe officer are seen in conversation at Poltava in October 1941 – soon after the Croatian *staffel* had arrived on the Eastern Front. The Bf 109E behind them bears the letter 'U' (for *Ustasa*) and a chalked 'Winged Croat shield', which became the official insignia of 15 (*Kroat*)./JG 52 in January 1942. This marking was subsequently carried on most of its aircraft (*HPM*)

Ivan Mrak, it comprised two units – 5. *Bombaska Skupina* (Bomber Group) with 154 men, and 4. *Zrakoplovna Lovacka Skupina* (ZLS – air force fighter group) with 202 men under the command of Major Franjo Dzal.

It should be noted that this was a Luftwaffe unit, for its members were obliged to take an oath of loyalty to the *Führer*, and it was under the direct command of the *Reichsluftfahrtministerium* (RLM). Personnel was also subject to German military law, and they wore Luftwaffe uniforms and were issued with German aircraft and servicing equipment.

Bomber personnel were sent to *Grosse Kampffliegerschüle* 3 at Greifswald on 19 July, while fighter pilots went to *Jagdfliegerschüle* 4 at Fürth, near Nüremberg, for just over two months' training. Students received instruction on Bücker Bu 133s, Arado Ar 96s and Messerschmitt Bf 109s.

There were some accidents during this time, with the most serious being the collision of Bf 109D-1 Wk-Nr 2605 and Bf 109B-1 Wk-Nr 390 on 12 August – both Stabsfeldwebel Safet Boskic and Oberleutnant Ivan Rubcic baled out, although Rubcic's parachute was not properly fastened and he died after falling from his harness. Ten days later Hauptmann Aksam Vid Tripmire wrecked Bf 109D Wk-Nr 2539 in an emergency landing at Kettingsworth. He was seriously injured and returned to Croatia.

Twenty-one pilots completed their training, allowing 10. and 11. *Zrakoplovno Lovacko Jato* (ZLJ – air force fighter squadron) to be formed. The unit commanders were Hauptleute Vladimir Ferencina and Zlatko Stipcic, respectively.

Pilots from 10. and 11.ZLJ were the first to leave for the front ahead of 4.ZLS, whose departure was postponed through insufficient equipment. Instead of the promised equipment of 24 Bf 109Es and one Bf 108, ten pilots (Majors Franjo Dzal and Mato Culinovic, Hauptleute Zlatko Stipcic and Vladimir Ferencina, Oberleutnante Ljudevit Bencetic, Albin Starc and Ivan Karner, Stabsfeldwebel Safet Boskic and Oberfeldwebeln Cvitan Galic and Tomislav Kauzlaric) and a *Verbindungsoffizier* (liaison officer Leutnant Ewald Baumgarten) left Fürth for the Ukraine on 28 September with just ten Bf 109Es and one Bf 109F.

Appropriately decorated 'hack' Bf 108B-2 'BD+JG' of 15 (*Kroat*). JG 52 was used on a daily basis for a variety of purposes (*HPM*)

The transfer took nine days to complete, and it was done in the following stages – Fürth–Prague/Kbely–Krakow–Lvov(Lemberg)–Vinica-Kirovgrad-Poltava. Only nine aircraft arrived, for two were destroyed near Biskovice during the first leg of the journey, resulting in the death of Oberleutnant Karner and the wounding of Major Culinovic. Another Bf 109 was damaged on landing at Lvov on 1 October.

The remaining pilots (Hauptleute Arkadije Popov, Berislav Supek and Josip Helebrant, Oberleutnante Ivan Jergovic, Nikola Vucina and Vilim Acinger, Stabsfeldwebel Stjepan Martinasevic, Oberfeldwebel Martin Korbelik, Feldwebeln Jure Lasta and Veca Mikovic and Unteroffizier Stjepan Radic) continued their training at Herzogen Aurah airfield, near Fürth, until 1 November. They then proceeded by train to the Soviet border and completed their journey by road to Mariupol, arriving on 16 December 1941.

COMBAT AT LAST

At Poltava, 150 km south-west of Harkov, 10.ZLJ was immediately subordinated to Major Hubertus von Bonin's III./JG 52, and designated 15(*Kroatische*)./JG 52.

On that section of the front, German and Romanian troops were advancing towards Rostov-on-Don, the Crimea and Kerch.

The unit flew its first combat mission on 9 October, and although Leutnant Ewald Baumgarten shot down a Kharkov R-10 reconnaissance bomber during the course of the sortie, his claim was not included in 15. *Staffel's* score. On 20 October, III./JG 52 transferred to the Crimea, although the Croatians remained at Poltava until the 27th. Eventually, on 12 November, they arrived at Taganrog airfield, before moving to Mariupol on 1 December.

Prior to embarking on these various base moves, the Croats had seen much action, as Albin Starc recounts;

'I flew in a *Schwarm* led by Stipcic, and we were escorting German twin-engined bombers. It was misty and cloudy, with bad visibility. We lost sight of the Germans and suddenly a bomber appeared from nowhere, straight in front of us. Stipcic fired immediately and broke to the side. We followed him, while the bomber, its engines smoking, dived into cloud. Stipcic reported his victory over the radio, and when he was over our airfield he rocked his wings.

'When we landed everybody was very excited, as word got around that we had achieved our "first". Soon afterwards a *Storch* landed and General Wolfram von Richthofen stepped out. We were lined up and he asked who the great shot had been. Stipcic proudly stepped forward – and received a hell of a dressing-down! It turned out that our "Russian" bomber was actually one of those we were supposed to escort. Luckily for Stipcic nobody was hurt, and the aircraft was barely damaged. After that he was removed from flying for six months on Richthofen's direct order.'

The legionnaires' first 'real' victories came on 2 November, when Hauptmann Ferencina and Leutnant Baumgarten each claimed a Polikarpov I-16 *Rata* near Rostov. Ferencina also encountered an unarmed biplane (probably a Polikarpov Po-2) over Soviet-held territory, and without firing a shot, he forced it to land. Ferencina then 'fired a burst away from the aircraft just to scare the pilot'.

Croatian ground personnel replenish cartridge belts for the Bf 109's 7.9 mm machine guns in harsh winter conditions. In fact, the winter of 1941-42 was one of the coldest of the 20th century in the Soviet Union, and Axis troops on the Eastern Front were completely unprepared for its severity (*HPM*)

On the 7th the unit's CO, Major Dzal, claimed another *Rata*. Two days later Oberfeldwebel Kauzlaric claimed a second I-16 – a victory which was not to be confirmed until the following spring. But there was more embarrassment on the way. After separating from his flight, Dzal returned jubilantly to base claiming to have downed four *Ratas* single-handedly. Croatian newspapers and radio made a lot of the story and congratulations poured in, but the Luftwaffe *Abschusskommision* (claims com-

mittee) refused to confirm more than four probables, since there had been no witnesses. Even intervention from the NDH high command could not change the decision.

Highly offended, Dzal was recalled to Croatia at the end of the year, and his deputy, Major Culinovic, took his place. Unofficial reports suggest that Dzal received confirmation for one of his kills in the spring of 1943, but no official documentation has been found to confirm this.

There was more success on 16 November when Oberleutnant Starc, Stabsfeldwebel Boskic and Leutnant Baumgarten were each credited with a *Rata*, while Stabsfeldwebel Galic claimed an unspecified enemy aircraft,

Future ace Albin Starc warms his hands on the exhaust pipes of an idling Bf 109E-7 during the winter of 1941–42 (*HPM*)

An airman helps Oberfahnrich Tomislav Kauzlaric strap on his parachute before commencing another sortie in 'Green 2'. The fighter's unusual camouflage was applied in an effort to make it less conspicuous when flying over the sea (*HPM*)

Aces Kauzlaric, Culinovic (in the white fur coat) and Starc are seen out on the snow in front of one of the unit's *Emils* in early 1942. The groundcrew are preparing the fighter for another sortie, although none of these pilots seem overly interested in taking the fighter aloft! Flying was severely reduced during the winter months because of the extremely low temperatures and the changeable nature of the weather. Evening taxying on the ground was fraught with danger, as Josip Helebrant remembers. 'The runway at Mariupol was effectively an ice passage, with huge layers of frozen snow on either side. The brakes were almost useless, and there were many accidents, especially on landing' (*L Javor*)

but this was unconfirmed. Four days later, Baumgarten died in a mid-air collision with another *Rata* near the village of Vlastovka. The destruction of the I-16 gave him his fifth victory. The last claimant of 1941 was Ferencina, who downed a *Rata* on 24 November.

By year's end, the unit had flown 50 combat missions and claimed five confirmed and six unconfirmed victories, one of which was later upgraded to a full kill. Its battle-strength, however, shrank rapidly. With replacement aircraft and spare parts arriving too slowly, only seven *Emils* – just three of them operational – were available by the end of 1941. Then, on 12 January 1942, 4.ZLS ceased to exist following an RLM order of 22 October 1941 that its units should be regrouped. Its personnel were duly incorporated into 10.*Ojacano* (Strengthened) ZLJ.

That winter the weather was bad, with temperatures plummeting to -39°C. Even the sea was frozen from December through to March. There

Pilots of 15 (*Kroat*)./JG 52 huddle together at Mariupol-Sud for a group photograph at the end of 1941. They are, from left to right, Stjepan Radic, Albin Starc (11 kills), Josip Helebrant (11 kills), Ljudevit Bencetic (15 kills), Berislav Supek, Martin Korbelik, Vladimir Ferencina (10 kills), Zlatko Stipcic (13 kills), Franjo Dzal (16 kills), Stjepan Martinasevic (11 kills), Mato Culinovic (12 kills), Ivan Jergovic (1 kill), Arkadije Popov, Cvitan Galic (38 kills), Nikola Vucina (2 kills), Veca Mikovic (12 kills) and Tomislav Kauzlaric (11 kills) (*J Novak*)

The pathetic remains of a Croatian Bf 109E which was destroyed by Soviet bombers at Mariupol during the winter of 1941–42. Soviet bombers constantly attacked the bases of 15(*Kroat*)./JG 52, although the most unpleasant raids were those made at night by Polikarpov Po-2 and R-5 biplanes (*L Javor*)

was very little aerial activity in January, although on New Year's Day an *Emil* suffered 40 per cent damage at Mariupol.

It was during this time that Hauptmann Arkadije Popov arrived at Mariupol with the second group of Croatian pilots, but as he was of Russian descent, his loyalty came under suspicion, leading to allegations that he was planning to defect to the Soviets. Popov was arrested by the *Gestapo* for interrogation, and after five months in jail he was handed over to the UNS – the *Ustasa* interrogation service. By August 1943 he had been imprisoned and released twice more, losing his left ear during torture. Popov, though, was a man of great physical and mental strength, for he not only survived but returned to the ZNDH, and eventually commanded 16.ZJ.

Then, on 23 October 1943 he escaped to Tortorella airfield, in Italy, in an ancient Breguet Br 19/8 and eventually joined the RAF's No 352 (Yugoslav) Sqn. He was subsequently killed on 16 October 1944 when his Spitfire Mk VC (JK447) was hit by flak near Slano, on the Dalmatian coast.

15(*Kroat*)./JG 52's first successful air combat of 1942 came on 9 February when Major Culinovic (in Bf 109E-7 Wk-Nr 1438) claimed two I-16s near Taganrog. Three days later, Stabsfeldwebel Boskic was injured when he crashed Bf 109E-7 Wk-Nr 7672. On 25 February, Oberstleutnant Dzal returned to take command of the unit.

With the advent of better weather, more Soviet aircraft appeared over the frontline during March, thus increasing the chances of aerial combat. On the 2nd of the month, while patrolling over the coast, Cvitan Galic (in Bf 109E-4 Wk-Nr 1285) claimed his first confirmed kill when he downed an R-10. He later described this action in a wartime magazine article;

'I went after the enemy – my first opponent – reminding myself of what I had learned in training. He is directly in my sights! My aircraft is flying level. Press the gun-button! The luminous trail of bullets goes straight to the target. By that time I have overtaken *Ivan*, who flies to my left. I turn, pursue the enemy again and fire. He falls in front of me! He crashes to earth, spurting little flames. At first I didn't feel any elation at my victory. I was just surprised, immensely surprised, that it had all happened so fast,

Cvitan Galic shot down this Kharkov R-10 on 2 March 1942. This large two-seat reconnaissance bomber dated from the mid-1930s, and was thoroughly obsolete at the time of Operation *Barbarossa* in June 1941, yet it remained in Soviet service well into 1942. Indeed, a significant number of virtually defenceless R-10s were claimed by Croatian fighter pilots (*J Novak*)

and that the Soviet pilot had not defended himself at all. I had downed my first enemy, but the joy of it came later.'

In fact Galic did not have time to celebrate, for minutes later he claimed a *Rata* probably destroyed near Margantovka. Three days later (in Bf 109E-7 Wk-Nr 1438) he claimed two more *Ratas*, while Feldwebel Jure Lasta (in Bf 109E-7 Wk-Nr 6087) downed another over Lisonogorskaya.

On the 8th Oberfeldwebel Stjepan Martinasevic (again in Bf 109E-7 Wk-Nr 6087) shot down a *Rata* that had attempted to intercept bombers near Matveyev Kurgan. Martinasevic repeated this feat on the 15th near Abramovka, this time in Bf 109E-7 Wk-Nr 6354. His wingman, Oberleutnant Ivan Jergovic, claimed his sole victory on this occasion. On the 16th, Lasta (in Bf 109-7 Wk-Nr 6124) and Galic (in Bf 109E-4 Wk-Nr 1285) again enjoyed success against the *Ratas* when each pilot claimed an I-16 during a *Freie Jagd* sweep near the village of Sinyavka.

During the afternoon of 20 March, Franjo Dzal (in Bf 109E-7 Wk-Nr 1438) led two of his pilots – Oberleutnant Nikola Vucina and Feldwebel Veca Mikovic (in Bf 109E-7 Wk-Nr 6087) – on a patrol. Whilst flying near Jurskoye Povod, Dzal downed a MiG-1, and a little later, over Borisoska, Vucina claimed another, while Mikovic destroyed two *Ratas*. The following morning five *Emils* flew over the front, where they arrived in time to help III./JG 52 engage *Ratas* and SB 2 bombers near Pokrovskoye. The Germans claimed two fighters and a bomber, and Mikovic (again in Bf 109E-7 Wk-Nr 6087) destroyed a third *Rata*.

The next morning Vucina shot down a Polikarpov I-153 *Chaika* near Uspenskaya village. Later that same day Dzal (in Bf 109E-7 Wk-Nr 1438), Feldwebel Mikovic and Unteroffizier Radic took off on a coastal patrol, but Radic was forced to turn back with engine trouble. Minutes later two SB-2s, and their MiG-1 escort, were encountered, and Dzal managed to damage the right engine of one of the Tupolev bombers. The solitary MiG pilot bravely engaged the Croats, hitting the cockpit, engine and propeller of Mikovic's Bf 109E-1 (Wk-Nr 2680), and effectively driving off the attack.

On the 24th *Staffel* pilots flew 14 sorties and claimed three kills. Lasta (in Bf 109E-1 Wk-Nr 950) got a *Rata* near Uspenskaya, Stjepan Radic claimed a MiG-1 near Taganrog and Mikovic (flying Wk-Nr 950 in its second sortie of the day) downed a second MiG in the same area.

During an early-morning mission the following day, Franjo Dzal endured a tense engagement which was described in the unit's diary:

'The assignment was to rendezvous with a reconnaissance aircraft near Matveyev Kurgan, but it did not arrive due to bad weather. Oberstleutnant Dzal and Feldwebel Mikovic continued to patrol the front, and at 0610 hrs they saw five I-153s and three I-16s. They immediately attacked. In his first pass, Oberstleutnant Dzal shot down an I-153. All the enemy machines

Wearing a life jacket around his neck, Oberfahnrich Cvitan Galic chats with his groundcrew whilst standing on the wing of Bf 109E-3 'Green 15' at Mariupol in the late spring of 1942. This aircraft was flown by a number of successful Croatian pilots, including Stipcic, Kauzlaric, Lasta and Galic, although it was primarily the mount of 12-kill ace Veca Mikovic (*J Novak*)

Major Mato Culinovic squeezes himself into battle-weary Bf 109E-7 'Green 29' during the late spring of 1942. The Croatian *Emils* were beginning to show their age by this stage of the campaign (*J Novak*)

carried 10-kg bombs, and when they saw our aircraft they jettisoned them on their own territory and attempted to escape. One aircraft landed, but it is not known why.

'Ten more modern enemy aircraft then approached us from behind and attacked our pair. We also came under heavy Russian ground fire. Oberstleutnant Dzal's aircraft was hit in the fuselage by a cannon shell, which damaged his radio. One machine-gun bullet hit the cockpit and another his propeller blade. Our pilots lost both radio and visual contact because of low cloud, although we all made it back to Taganrog airfield uninjured.'

Although April 1942 proved less successful in terms of the number of communist aircraft shot down, it nevertheless saw the HZL produce its first aces. At 0600 hrs on the 7th, Hauptmann Acinger, Fahnrich Galic and Feldwebel Mikovic commenced a *Freie Jagd* sweep. They soon encountered a mixed formation of Soviet fighters, and Veca Mikovic (in Bf 109E-7 Wk-Nr 6087) claimed a MiG-3 for his fifth victory south-east of Dyakovo village, as did Cvitan Galic (in Bf 109E-4 Wk-Nr 1285) when he downed a *Chaika* just moments later. By month's end, five more *Ratas*, three Ilyushin DB-3 bombers, a Yak UT-2 and three probables had been claimed.

By order of General Kren, another reorganisation – on paper at least – occurred on 16 April when 4.ZLS was re-established, led by Franjo Dzal. Mato Culinovic and Vladimir Ferencina were put in charge of 10. and 11.ZLJ respectively. According to ZNDH documents, 4.ZLS would undergo more internal changes later in the war, but during its time on the Eastern Front its official RLM-designation was always 15*(Kroat)./* JG 52. When led by Franjo Dzal it was also unofficially nicknamed *Jagdgruppe* 'Dzal'.

On 24 April, Bf 109E-7 Wk-Nr 6087 was destroyed on the ground by Soviet bombers. The Croatians suffered their first pilot loss of 1942 when, on the 27th, Hauptmann Berislav Supek got lost and landed his Bf 109E-3 ('Green 4' Wk-Nr 1411) on a Red Army-held airfield near Rostov. After the war, in communist Yugoslavia, he claimed to have defected.

Before joining the VVKJ Supek had been a member of the Yugoslav Communist Youth, yet in 1937 he had shown himself to be fervently anti-communist when he became a member of the *Ustasa*. After 're-education' by the Soviet NKVD, he changed his affinity once more, and his devotion to communism proved to be so strong that when Yugoslavia broke its ties with the Soviet Union in 1948, Supek defected to Rumania. He eventually returned home in the 1960s.

On 2 May the unit moved from Mariupol to Sarabusi and Eupatoria airfields. From here, 4.ZLS flew a series of *jabo* (fighter-bomber) missions against enemy positions in Sevastopol. The following day Hauptmann Ferencina was shot down and wounded during a clash with a formation of Soviet fighters.

4 May saw the first true desertion take place when Oberleutnant Nikola Vucina flew over to the Soviets in Bf 109E-7 'Green 9' (Wk-Nr 1506). In 1946, he switched sides again when he piloted a Po-2 to Italy!

Further base relocation took place on the 17th, 4.ZLS moving to Artemovsk and Konstantinovka, before returning to Mariupol 12 days later. During this period there were few opportunities for the legionnaires to add to their scores, and only six confirmed and three unconfirmed kills were claimed during the entire month of May.

Kauzlaric, flying Bf 109E-4 Wk-Nr 1618, claimed a *Rata* near Lisinogorskaya on 5 May, and 15 days later Zlatko Stipcic, in 'Green 10', opened his score in the east with a MiG-3 and a DB-3F. That same day Galic, Starc and Kauzlaric each claimed an aircraft apiece over Sevastopol.

Despite these successes, the *Emils* being flown by 4.ZLS were beginning to show their age. Three were written off in accidents in May – Bf 109E-7s Wk-Nrs 4217 and 5058 and Bf 109E-4 Wk-Nr 1285. To fill these gaps, the RLM sent the unit a

Brothers in arms: Vladimir Ferencina and an unknown sailor serving with the Croat Naval Legion pose together somewhere in the Crimea in the spring of 1942 (*S Ostric*)

Mechanics examine the engine of an *Emil* at Eupatoria airfield in the spring of 1942. The serviceability of 15(*Kroat*)./JG 52 aircraft was worsening at this time, which was hardly surprising as these Bf 109Es had been in constant combat for two years. Indeed, they had seen action with various Luftwaffe units all over Europe, and some had even served as far afield as North Africa with JG 27 (*HPM*)

Mechanics report the status of this *Emil* to a smartly dressed Vladimir Ferencina at Eupatoria in the early spring of 1942. Ferencina was wounded in action in Bf 109E-4 Wk-Nr 3664 near Sevastopol on 3 May 1942, the ace managing to coax his battle-damaged fighter back to Sarabusi airfield, where he wrecked it in a crash-landing (*S Ostric*)

Bf 109E-4 'Green 5' is tended at Eupatoria in May 1942. Ace Albin Starc was one of the pilots who frequently used this *Emil* (*J Novak*)

few more war-weary *Emils* from *Reparaturszentern*, some of which had previously been used by JG 27 in North Africa! Despite these replacements, *Staffel* strength at this time never exceeded eight operational aircraft. Things got worse in early June when a take-off collision between two aircraft resulted in Bf 109E-4 Wk-Nr 1483 being written off. In less than two weeks, five more *Emils* were badly damaged in accidents.

Yet the Croats remained effective in air combat, with eight more claims being submitted by 20 June. On that day, Galic claimed a MiG-1 for his tenth confirmed kill. Starc downed a *Rata* and Mikovic, in 'Green 15', two MiGs – these were the unit's 50th and 51st confirmed victories. The next day, the pilots of 4.ZLS flew their 1,000th combat mission, and scored their 52nd kill. One of those men to see much action during this period was Hauptmann Josip Helebrant, who fought several battles with MiG-3s in the second half of June. Indeed, he reported damaging MiGs on 18, 24 and 27 June, and one of these was later confirmed as his first victory.

By this time most other Luftwaffe units were operating Bf 109Fs and even early versions of the *Gustav*, leaving HZL pilots to voice their dissatisfaction with their old *Emils*. Croatian demands for modern aircraft became louder once they had proven their skills, and finally, on 3 June,

Still wearing his life jacket, Hauptmann Stipcic gives Oberfahnrich Kauzlaric a graphic account of his aerial engagement over Sevastopol on 20 May 1942. Both pilots were successful on that day, Stipcic claiming a MiG-3 and a DB-3F, while Kauzlaric accounted for a second MiG fighter (*S Ostric*)

Josip Helebrant poses for the camera whilst taking a close look at a captured MiG-3 at Simferopol shortly after returning from leave in early April 1942. The aircraft had been captured by Rumanian troops. The first mass-produced MiG fighter, the MiG-3 was no match for the Bf 109 at medium to low level, and the Croats downed a large number of them (*J Novak*)

The work of Mato Culinovic – 'Green 7' stands on its nose at Mariupol in June 1942. Culinovic had several similar accidents in various *Emils* at around this time! (*J Novak*)

Franjo Dzal went to Berlin to lodge an official complaint via the ZNDH Attaché, ppuk Marijan Dolanski. Twelve days later a group of pilots from 4.ZLS left for Uman to gain experience with the Bf 109G-2. The first *Gustav* arrived at Mariupol on 1 July, and by the end of the month 14 were on the unit's strength.

During its time with the *Emil*, 15(Kroat)./JG 52 had flown 1,115 sorties, of which 265 were interceptions, 134 escort, 60 airfield protection, 58 patrol, 30 *Freie Jagd*, 32 low-level attacks, 50 *jabo* and 52 reconnaissance missions. Between 9 October 1941 and 6 July 1942, 60 to 66 confirmed and 11 to 13 unconfirmed kills were achieved, three aircraft destroyed on the ground and four badly damaged. Two Croatian pilots had been lost and three wounded.

After the fall of Sevastopol on 1 July, aerial activity became more intense. On the 4th Helebrant and Radic attacked shipping and the former sank a patrol boat near Jeysk.

The legionnaires soon felt at home with their new Bf 109Gs, and 13 claims were made on 9-10 July alone, with Galic claiming three kills, Stipcic, Starc and Bencetic two each, Dzal a DB-3F for his fifth confirmed kill and Culinovic, Ferencina and Mikovic one apiece.

Bf 109G-2 Wk-Nr 13421 became the first 15(Kroat)./JG 52 *Gustav* to be lost in action when it was shot down by anti-aircraft fire on the 9th. Three days later a *Rotte* (probably comprising Culinovic and Stipcic) claimed three fighters and three bombers during a single mission. On the 13th Helebrant, Starc and Mikovic fought three *Ratas*, with the latter pilot downing one and Helebrant's fighter being slightly damaged.

THE OPPOSITION

Air combat in the east during 1941–42 was marked by great inequality. On the Axis side were seasoned Luftwaffe veterans who

The rudder of Cvitan Galic's last *Emil* displays his scoreboard. With 11 confirmed and three unconfirmed kills, he was the most successful Croat pilot with the Bf 109E, closely followed by Veca Mikovic with eight plus two. Note the precarious attitude of the *Emil* in the background (*J Novak*)

Still wearing his flying helmet, Hauptmann Ferencina emerges from the cockpit of 'Green 15' to be surrounded by groundcrew upon his return from a successful mission on a sunny day in June 1942 (*S Ostric*)

were ably supported by less experienced, but nevertheless well-trained, pilots flying superb modern fighters. Opposing them were a handful of Soviet pilots who had lived long enough to gain the skills necessary for survival, but who were backed up by literally thousands of young and inexperienced trainees flying obsolete aircraft, and employing outmoded tactics. Any attempt to show initiative or criticise how the air war was being run could lead to immediate transfer to punishment squadrons, the first rows of infantry trenches or, worse still, NKVD death-squads.

Many HZL veterans considered it quite easy to score victories during this period, as Josip Helebrant remembers;

'Flak was what really scared us, especially from ships. Russian fighters were no match for us. The hardest thing was to find an enemy aircraft to shoot down, and we were not the only ones searching. Once you had found one, the only thing to do was to approach, aim, fire a short burst and break. It was the same whether it was an SB, a *Rata* or a MiG. Real dogfights, with twisting and turning where you could show what you really knew, were quite rare. It seemed as if the only thing these poor lads learned was how to take off, fly straight and land. I felt real pity for them. But it was war, and war is always an unfair game.'

There were times when fighter pilots suppressed their predatory instincts in favour of more humane feelings, as Albin Starc, who flew with Safet 'Slavko' Boskic during the summer of 1942, recalls:

'Our patrol had been quite uneventful, and as we prepared to head back to our airfield, "Slavko" saw a lone LaGG flying straight and level at low altitude. He quickly positioned himself for an attack, but for some reason didn't shoot. Instead, he flew alongside the Russian. He looked at the pilot and saw a blond chap in his late teens without a flying helmet just staring at him, paralysed. He waved and broke off. After we landed, I asked him why he had let him go, and he replied, "I couldn't kill a kid".'

A mechanic works on the engine of recently arrived Bf 109G-2 'Black 8' while his friend catches up on his sleep in the shade of the port wing. Two weary *Emils* ('Green 9' and '11') can be seen parked in the background. These veteran fighters remained in HZL service for a month after the arrival of the first *Gustavs* in early July 1942 (*HPM*)

On 20 July Oberfeldwebel Veca Mikovic became separated from his *Schwarm* while chasing a lone Petlyakov Pe-2 bomber. His Bf 109G-2 ('Black 13' Wk-Nr 13411) was hit by return fire, which started a fuel leak. Mikovic tried to reach the safety of his own lines, but was killed when he crashed in no-man's land near Rostov.

On the next sortie Tomislav Kauzlaric saw Josip Helebrant shoot down another Pe-2, which crashed into the sea near Yeysk. Two days later, Axis forces launched an offensive aimed at capturing the oil fields in the Caucasus. The aerial battles in support of this campaign would continue well into 1943.

Ljudevit Bencetic escaped serious injury on 24 July when his Bf 109G-2 ('Black 9' Wk-Nr 13489) crashed on take-off. The next day Major Ferencina claimed a MiG-3 near Chorbinovskaya, and two minutes later Major Culinovic repeated the feat.

The *Staffel* moved from Mariupol to Taganrog on the 26th, and the following day Dzal ('Black 1') and Galic ('Black 3') encountered six LaGG-3s while on a *Freie Jagd*. They each claimed a kill apiece, both

Mato Culinovic leans on the door of the 'official' *Staffel* car – note the 'winged Croat shield' on the mudguard – in the summer of 1942 (*S Ostric*)

fighters falling in German-held territory near Podaysk.

But the unit almost lost its CO on 28 July. Franjo Dzal and Vladimir Ferencina were on a *Freie Jagd* between Rostov and Bataysk, when they were attacked by numerous Soviet fighters. Dzal's 'Black 1' (Wk-Nr 13436) was hit in the engine, and he crash-landed behind enemy lines near the village of Shamshiyev. Evading capture, Dzal crossed back into German-held territory a few hours later.

The *Staffel* was soon on the move again, arriving in Rostov on the 29th, Bjelaja Glina on 7 August and Armavir three days later.

The new month opened with more success, when Galic ('Black 3') and Starc ('Black 2') each claimed a LaGG-3 on the 7th following a clash with five Soviet fighters over Novo Pokrovskoye. There was much jubilation 24 hours later when Helebrant, flying 'Black 8', downed a DB-3 near Armavir, the bomber crashing in flames. This was the unit's 100th confirmed victory.

Further successes were not long in coming, for on the 13th Galic ('Black 3') and Martinasevic ('Black 9') took off on a *Freie Jagd* sweep over the Maikop area. They engaged a formation of *Chaikas* and Galic claimed one west of Neftogorsk, while his wingman downed two more. The following day, Helebrant belly-landed his 'Black 8' (Wk-Nr 13463) at Armavir airfield when its hydraulic pump failed.

During an early-morning Stuka escort mission to Novorossiysk on 16 August, Fahnrich Galic ('Black 3') and Stabsfeldwebel Boskic ('Black 10') each claimed a MiG-3. Three days later, while on a *Freie Jagd* sweep, Fahnrich Kauzlaric ('Black 6') downed a *Chaika* near Gostojevskaja, and on the 20th Oberleutnant Starc ('Black 5') destroyed a LaGG-3. Just before noon on 24 August, a *Rotte* comprising Starc ('Black 2') and

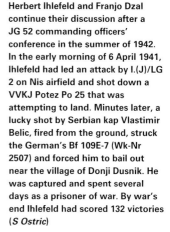

Herbert Ihlefeld and Franjo Dzal continue their discussion after a JG 52 commanding officers' conference in the summer of 1942. In the early morning of 6 April 1941, Ihlefeld had led an attack by I.(J)/LG 2 on Nis airfield and shot down a VVKJ Potez Po 25 that was attempting to land. Minutes later, a lucky shot by Serbian kap Vlastimir Belic, fired from the ground, struck the German's Bf 109E-7 (Wk-Nr 2507) and forced him to bail out near the village of Donji Dusnik. He was captured and spent several days as a prisoner of war. By war's end Ihlefeld had scored 132 victories (*S Ostric*)

Hauptmann Helebrant arrives back at Armavir on 8 August 1942, having just scored 15(*Kroat*)./JG 52's 100th confirmed victory (*S Ostric*)

Eleven-kill ace Oberfeldwebel Stjepan Martinasevic poses by the nose of his remarkably clean *Emil* at Eupatoria in May 1942 (*S Ostric*)

Hauptmann Ferencina is helped on with his parachute harness prior to flying a sortie in Bf 109G-2/R6 'Black 11'. The ten-kill ace enjoyed an eventful two weeks in August 1942, for on the 19th this very fighter (Wk-Nr 13517) caught fire in flight, although Ferencina managed to return to Kertch. Two days later he crash-landed 'Black 10' (Wk-Nr 13438). Ferencina then claimed an SB-2 on the 25th, but the following day he force-landed in the steppe near Krimskaya after flak struck his 'Black 1' (Wk-Nr 13577). Finally, on the 27th, the ace wrote off 'Black 11' in a take-off accident (*S Ostric*)

Oberfahnrich Kauzlaric sits on the wing of Bf 109G-6/R6 'Black 9' at Armavir. On 29 August 1942 fellow ace Feldwebel Stjepan Radic was killed in this aircraft when he attempted to force-land the battle-damaged fighter near Tuapse. Note the *Gustav's* under wing cannon gondolas and unusual spinner marking (*HPM*)

Kauzlaric ('Black 6') encountered Soviet bombers and escorts near Novorossiysk, Starc claiming a LaGG-3, and Kauzlaric a DB-3.

The Croatian pilots were particularly busy on 29 August, flying 20 combat sorties. During the first of these, which began at dawn, Kauzlaric ('Black 6') shot down a MiG-3 which Oberleutnant Bencetic saw crash. But the *Staffel's* youngest pilot was to be killed on the next patrol in the same area. Feldwebel Stjepan Radic had just claimed an Il-2 *Stormovik* when flak punctured the glycol tank of his 'Black 9' (Wk-Nr 13520). He tried to reach friendly territory but lost height steadily. Radic then attempted a force-landing, and Zlatko Stipcic watched in horror as 'Black 9' crashed and exploded after hitting tree-tops.

There was no time for grieving, however, as the next mission took off at 0700 hrs. During the course of the flight Helebrant claimed another *Stormovik* east of Shirvanskaya. Next day, during an early-morning Focke-Wulf Fw 189 escort mission, Franjo Dzal ('Black 13') claimed an Il-2 and a MiG-3, with a second Mikoyan fighter falling to Stjepan Martinasevic ('Black 7'). The final kill of the month fell to the guns of Cvitan Galic when he claimed a MiG-3 during a close-support sortie in the Novorossiysk–Anapa area.

It was during this period that the *Wehrmacht* fought a bitter battle on

the Novorossiysk front, with the Croatian *Staffel* being one of the units providing air support in the form of hundreds of *Freie Jagd* (averaging 20 escort missions per day). The victory tally mounted steadily, with Galic heading the unit's scoreboard. His first kill of the campaign came during an early morning patrol on 1 September when he claimed a MiG-3 near Novorossiysk.

Tomislav Kauzlaric and Josip Helebrant chat at Mariupol in the spring of 1942. A Croatian *Emil* can be seen in the distance (*S Ostric*)

Two days later, while escorting an Fw 189, Starc ('Black 12') and Martinasevic ('Black 11') fought eight *Ratas* near Novorossiysk, damaging two of them – Martinasevic's claim was subsequently confirmed. On 4 September, during similar missions in the same area, Hauptmann Helebrant ('Black 8') claimed a LaGG-3 and Galic ('Black 3') a MiG-3.

Early on the 6th, Martinasevic ('Black 7') downed an unidentified enemy aircraft near Krivenkoskaya station, while Helebrant and Starc strafed a 100-ton tanker, which capsized after its cargo exploded. Three hours later a *Schwarm* covering an Fw 189 encountered six DB-3s and five escorting fighters west of Novorossiysk. In a prolonged battle, Oberleutnant Bencetic ('Black 5') claimed a bomber destroyed, but this was not witnessed by the other pilots.

On the afternoon of the following day, three *Gustavs* took off from Yelisavetinskaya airfield on a patrol, and whilst aloft Helebrant, in his

Leutnant Dragutin Ivanic, the non-flying toohnical ufficer of 15(*Kroat*)./JG 52, is seen sat in front of 'Black 8'. The solitary white victory bar that adorns the fighter's tail is attributed to Hauptmann Helebrant. Some historians have mistakenly credited Ivanic with no less than 18 victories, despite the fact that he never learned to fly! (*J Novak*)

Josip Helebrant poses beside the nose of 'Black 8' at Maikop airfield in the autumn of 1942. Helebrant claimed eight kills flying this aircraft, seven of which were confirmed (*S Ostric*)

usual 'Black 8', claimed a *Rata*. On 8 September Helebrant (again in 'Black 8') and Martinasevic ('Black 7') took-off to patrol Novorossiysk. Once over the frontline, they encountered 11 *Chaikas* escorting a Polikarpov R-5 observation biplane. In the ensuing dogfight they jointly accounted for the R-5, and Martinasevic also got a *Chaika*.

On returning to base, the victorious pilots tossed a coin to decide which of them would get credit for the R-5. Helebrant won to take full credit for what he described in his logbook as the 'big biplane'.

Four hours later, three patrolling *Gustavs* attacked a mixed formation of three DB-3s and ten *Ratas* near Gelendzhik. Martinasevic, now in 'Black 4', claimed one of the bombers. The day's score was closed by Galic ('Black 12') and Lasta ('Black 11') when, during a patrol east of Novorossiysk shortly after 1530 hrs, they each shot down a *Chaika*. The Soviets extracted some revenge the next day when they damaged Galic's 'Black 12' (Wk-Nr 13654), forcing him to crash-land at Krimskaya airfield.

During the evening of 10 September, Helebrant ('Black 10') and Lasta ('Black 11') encountered a massive formation of Soviet fighters and six DB-3s over the city of Novorossiysk. Helebrant managed to bring one bomber down before the escorts damaged his aircraft.

The following day four *Gustavs* left Yelisavetinskaya to patrol the Novorossiysk–Gelendzhik road, where they engaged five *Chaikas* and 14 *Ratas*. Oberstleutnant Dzal (in 'Black 1' Wk-Nr 13577) shot down one of each type, and Fahnrich Kauzlaric ('Black 6') also got a *Rata*. However, Dzal was bounced by one of the I-16s and his Messerschmitt struck in the wings, tail and engine. Despite damage to the radiator and oil cooler, he returned safely. During the same mission Helebrant ('Black 10') was hit by German flak, and he barely managed to force land safely at Abinskaya auxiliary airfield with his engine on fire.

Almost a year in the frontline had sapped both the mental and physical strength of the Croatian pilots. Their ranks thinned by constant combat,

Oberstleutnant Franjo Dzal returns from a mission in Bf 109G-2 Wk-Nr 13577 'Black 1' in August 1942. Although the CO's personal aircraft, this machine was also flown by Kauzlaric, Boskic, Ferencina, Starc and Bencetic on numerous occasions (*HPM*)

Oberleutnant Albin Starc looks pleased after ferrying this recently built Bf 109G-2 from Uman to Jelisavetinskaya during the second half of August 1942. HZL markings have still to be added (*Authors*)

the unit had also had to battle with disease and infection as well. By early September 1942 only nine combat-ready pilots remained.

To keep 15.*Staffel* operational until the arrival of new pilots from training schools in Germany, five Luftwaffe pilots from II./JG 52 (Leutnant Fritz and Feldwebeln Bormichel, Rabiega, Schmohr and Scholze), along with their aircraft, were attached to it by order of IV *Fliegerkorps* on 12 September. But after just six days, during which time the German pilots flew 38 sorties, the order was changed and they returned to their *Gruppe*.

On 23 September, the *Wehrmacht's* 17th *Armee* started a push towards Tuapse. After sustaining heavy losses (by 1 October, the 5th Air Army had just 120 aircraft, including 52 fighters) the Soviets scaled back their opposition to the assault.

At 1655 hrs on the 25th, a stand-by *Rotte* scrambled to intercept four *Stormoviks* of 502.ShAP that had been detected heading for Maikop airfield. Galic shot one down south of Shadishemskaya and a German pilot accounted for another. One of the downed aircraft was flown by future Hero of the Soviet Union Lt Grigoriy K Kochergin, who evaded capture and returned to his unit after eight days (for a detailed description of Soviet Air Force ranks and organisation, see *Aircraft of the Aces 15 —Soviet Aces of World War 2*).

On the last day of the month, Franjo Dzal (Black 1) and Safet Boskic (Black 9) fought a group of LaGG-3s over Shadishemskaya, Dzal claiming two and Boskic one.

On 1 October, Lasta (in 'Black 4') claimed a 'MiG-3' east of Tuapse, but as there were no MiG units in this area at the time, his victim may have been a Yak-1, a Yak-7B or a LaGG-3. Two days later, during one of 27 sorties flown by the *Staffel*, Galic claimed his 20th victory – a Pe-2 – which was seen by his wingman Lasta to crash west of Atamish hill.

At 1017 hrs on the 6th, Helebrant (in 'Black 8' Wk-Nr 13463) and Starc ('Black 10') took off on a *Freie Jagd*, during which they surprised four *Stormoviks* of 502.ShAP, escorted by four LaGG-3s of 246.IAP, over the Pshish river. Helebrant claimed an Il-2 and Starc 'a Yak or LaGG'. According to Soviet sources, the *Stormovik* of Ser K M Lobanov was shot down, and two more were damaged, one of which was written off.

Leading a quartet of 518.IAP Yak 1s in the same area was Kap Sergey S Shchirov (a Soviet ace with at least 13 kills), and he saw the two Croatian Bf 109s attacking the Ilyushins below him. Shchirov dived on them, attacking 'Black 8'. He claimed that it crashed near Gunay mountain after his third attack, although in reality both *Gustavs* returned to Maikop. Admittedly, Helebrant's left hand had been slightly wounded by shrapnel, and his aircraft damaged. Their initial attack on the Il-2s had been so swift that the escorting LaGGs had not intervened, so it seems likely that Starc had claimed Shchirov's Yak in return.

The *Staffel* diary and German documents both state that three days later Franjo Dzal, with Oberfahnrich Tomislav Kauzlaric as his wingman, met three SB-2 bombers and their four escorting LaGG-3s near Komlovina. During the course of the engagement Kauzlaric was wounded but managed to return to Maikop, where he later recalled:

'After an inconclusive fight with the Russians we saw some Ju 88s returning home in loose formation with a few aircraft damaged. As we had nothing else to do, we approached to provide an escort. As I came close to one bomber, its gunner opened fire and I was hit twice in the right leg and once in the left arm by 7.9 mm bullets. The wounds weren't serious, but were quite complicated, and required lengthy treatment.

'I returned to Russia in May 1943, but my wounds had no totally healed, so before long I was sent back to Croatia for further recuperation. Anyway, that was my last sortie with the Legion.'

On 23 October Galic ('Black 10') and Lasta ('Black 11') engaged Soviet fighters, Lasta claiming what was believed to have been a MiG-3 near Lazarevskoye and Galic a *Rata*. The unit's 150th victory came two days later when, at 0752 hrs, Josip Helebrant (Black 8) and Albin Starc ('Black 4') took off on what was to be a successful *Freie Jagd* sweep of the Tuapse area. When they landed an hour later, each reported shooting down two LaGG-3s. Their victims were from 269.IAP, which was conducting its first mission in-theatre.

The Russians had planned for four LaGGs to fly close escort to four 502.ShAP Il-2s at 4800 ft (1500 m), with three more fighters above them and another three flying top cover at 6500 ft (2000 m). However, the

Second-ranking Croatian ace Cvitan Galic enjoys a cigarette alongside 'Black 3', which was his regular mount throughout the summer and autumn of 1942. The aircraft was also occasionally flown by Bencetic, Kauzlaric, Stipcic, Boskic, Starc, Dzal and Dukovac (*HPM*)

mid-section was unfamiliar with the area, and after getting lost, it aborted the mission. This left the low section exposed, and the Croat pilots pulled off a perfect bounce.

Two LaGGs were shot down in the first pass, St Lt Petr B Dolbnin being killed and Ser P D Malishev forced to bail out. Kap Pavel A Bichkov's aircraft was also seriously damaged and duly written off when he crash-landed at Lazarevskoye airfield. St Lt P S Popov engaged the *Gustavs* but later reported that his LaGG had been hit by Soviet flak during the dogfight, forcing him to bail out over the sea near Tihonovka. In the afternoon Lasta ('Black 11') claimed a MiG-3 near Tuapse, as did Galic ('Black 3') the following morning. On 24 October three *Gustavs* scrambled to intercept Pe-2 bombers approaching Maikop airfield, and Franjo Dzal in his 'Black 1' shot one down.

There was more heavy fighting for the *Staffel* on the 28th. During the first of eight missions flown that day, Lasta and Galic (on a *Freie Jagd*) encountered some LaGG-3s, and each claimed one. However, on his return flight Lasta's engine (in 'Black 16') suddenly exploded, and the aircraft dropped like a stone. The pilot had no chance of escaping, and he was killed when the Bf 109 hit the ground and exploded.

A little later, Dzal ('Black 1'), Galic and Bencetic ('Black 5') sortied as escorts for Ju 87s heading for Georgiyevskoye. As Soviet fighters tried to intercept the dive-bombers, they were jumped by the Croats, Dzal getting two LaGG-3s and Galic and Bencetic a MiG-3 apiece.

New Pilots

Back in the summer of 1941, 30 pilots with some VVKJ flying experience were selected for training and sent to *Flugzeugführerschüle* A/B 120

Croatian cadets are seen in formal pose at Prenzlau in June 1942. They are (standing), from left to right, Viktor Mihelcic, Drago Pavlicevic, Dragutin Sokol, Luka Kirola, Juraj Tomsic, Nikola Tosic, Milan Kucinic, Jozo Martinovic, Dragutin Misic, Bozidar Bartulovic, Hasib Dizdarevic and Josip Cipic. Seated, from left to right, Andjel Antic, Josip Nikoljacic (Yugoslav), Bogomir Rumler, Marko Bogdanovic, Ratimir Slavetic, Mato Dukovac and Sime Fabijanovic (*J Novak*)

at Prenzlau. Of the group, eight converted onto fighters, seven were chosen for bombers, 13 were 'washed out' and two died in accidents. The future fighter pilots had completed their supplementary training by mid June 1942, whereupon they were sent to *Jagdfliegerschüle* 4 at Fürth.

By October Leutnante Mato Dukovac, Josip Nikoljacic, Nikola Vice and Andjelko Antic, Oberfeldwebel Josip Cipic, Feldwebeln Viktor Mihelcic and Bozidar Bartulovic and Unteroffizier Dragomir Misic were ready to join their countrymen at the front.

On 29 October, a *Rotte* comprising Boskic ('Black 11') and Bencetic

Legionnaires received a heroes' welcome upon their return to Croatia, being awarded many honours. These distinguished aces are seen receiving decorations at a ceremony in Zagreb on 23 December 1942. They are, from the left, Dzal, Helebrant (receiving his decoration from by General Begic), Starc and Galic (*S Ostric*)

('Black 3') was scrambled to intercept Soviet fighters, and in a low level dogfight the veteran Croat pilots shot down two LaGG-3s. Later that day it was the turn of the newcomers to make their first 15-minute familiarisation flights in Bf 109G-2 'Black 5', and by the afternoon they were able to fly over the front as wingmen to experienced pilots. But one of the new arrivals was destined not to survive for long. The following day, when on only his second combat flight, Leutnant Josip Nikoljacic was shot down and killed in Bf 109G-2 'Black 10' (Wk-Nr 13608) when he was jumped by Soviet fighters west of Tuapse.

On 3 November, Fahnrich Galic and Leutnant Vice scrambled to intercept seven *Chaikas* and eight LaGG-3s, and on this occasion the Soviet pilots proved to be harder nuts to crack, damaging Galic's Bf 109G-2 ('Black 15' Wk-Nr 13445) south-east of Georgiyevskoye. He managed to crash-land the stricken fighter at Maikop-Nord airfield. His assailant was probably Lt Georgiy V Bessonov from 269.IAP, who reportedly shot down the leader of a pair of Bf 109s that day. The Soviets immediately dubbed him an 'ace', although this was in fact only his first kill.

Flying his 12th combat mission on 11 November, the man who would eventually emerge as the top-scoring Croatian pilot of the war at last began to show his skill. Leutnant Mato Dukovac and his element leader, Oberleutnant Bencetic, were escorting Stukas to Lazarevskoye when they were intercepted by *Ratas*. In the ensuing fight, Dukovac (in 'Black 11') claimed his first confirmed victory.

After a year of constant fighting, rumours that the Croat pilots were due to be rested and returned to Croatia were confirmed. They handed their aircraft over to II./JG 52 and began their homeward journey on 15 November. By then the pilots of 15(*Kroat*)./JG 52 had flown 3698 sorties, 2460 of which were combat missions – 533 escort, 151 airfield defence, 116 low-level attack and 65 *Jabo* missions. The unit had claimed 164 confirmed and 43 to 47 unconfirmed victories, 14 of which were later upgraded to full kills. In return, four Croatian pilots and five groundcrewmen had been killed, and a further two pilots were missing in action.

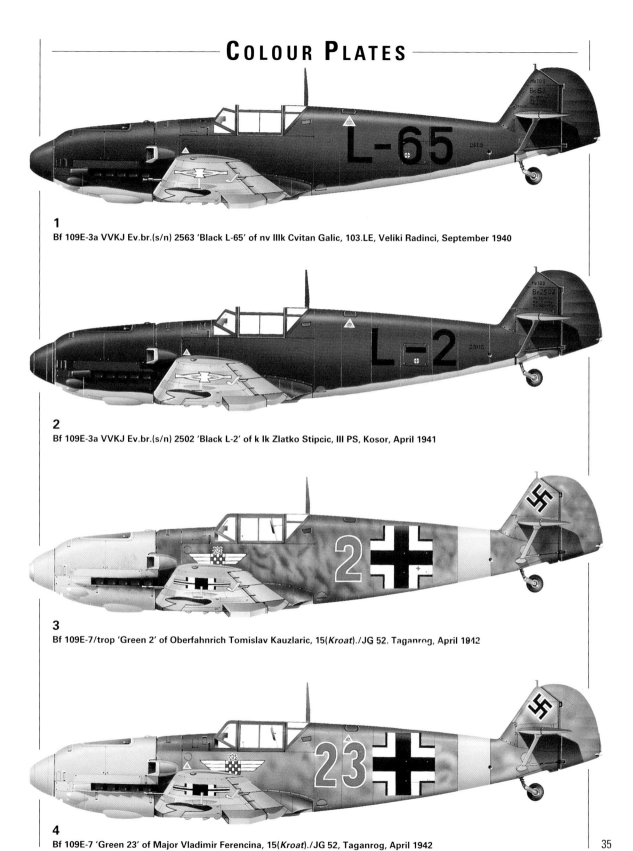

1
Bf 109E-3a VVKJ Ev.br.(s/n) 2563 'Black L-65' of nv IIIk Cvitan Galic, 103.LE, Veliki Radinci, September 1940

2
Bf 109E-3a VVKJ Ev.br.(s/n) 2502 'Black L-2' of k Ik Zlatko Stipcic, III PS, Kosor, April 1941

3
Bf 109E-7/trop 'Green 2' of Oberfahnrich Tomislav Kauzlaric, 15(*Kroat*)./JG 52, Taganrog, April 1942

4
Bf 109E-7 'Green 23' of Major Vladimir Ferencina, 15(*Kroat*)./JG 52, Taganrog, April 1942

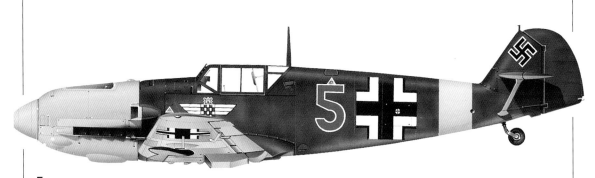

5
Bf 109E-4 'Green 5' of Oberleutnant Albin Starc, 15(*Kroat*)./JG 52, Eupatoria, May 1942

6
Bf 109E-3 'Green 15' of Major Vladimir Ferencina, 15(*Kroat*)./JG 52, Eupatoria, June 1942

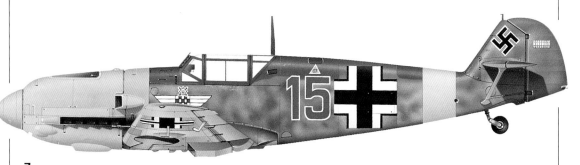

7
Bf 109E-3 'Green 15' of Oberfeldwebel Veca Mikovic, 15(*Kroat*)./JG 52, Mariupol, June 1942

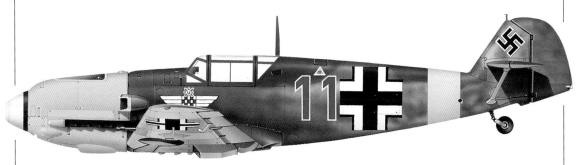

8
Bf 109E-3 'Green 11' of Major Mato Culinovic, 15(*Kroat*)./JG 52, Mariupol, July 1942

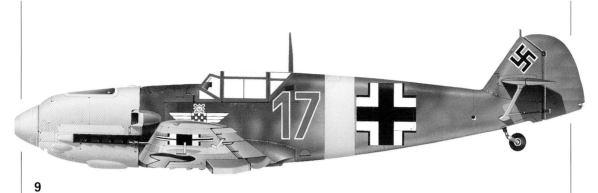

9
Bf 109E-3 'Green 17' of Feldwebel Stjepan Radic, 15(*Kroat*)./JG 52, Mariupol, July 1942

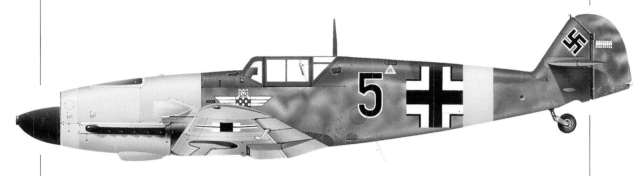

10
Bf 109G-2 'Black 5' of Oberleutnant Ljudevit Bencetic, 15(*Kroat*)./JG 52, Mariupol, July 1942

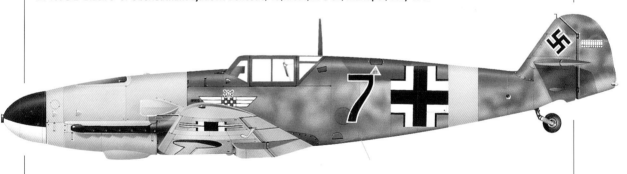

11
Bf 109G-2 'Black 7' of Major Mato Culinovic, 15(*Kroat*)./JG 52, Mariupol, July 1942

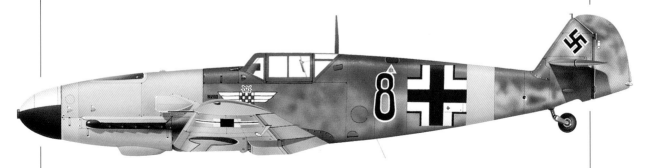

12
Bf 109G-2 Wk-Nr 13463 'Black 8' of Hauptmann Josip Helebrant, 15(*Kroat*)./JG 52, Mariupol, July 1942

13
Bf 109G-2/R6 Wk-Nr 13520 'Black 9' of Oberfeldwebel Stjepan Martinasevic, 15(*Kroat*)./JG 52, Armavir, August 1942

14
Bf 109G-2 Wk-Nr 13438 'Black 10' of Oberfahnrich Safet Boskic, 15(*Kroat*)./JG 52, Kertch, August 1942

15
Bf 109G-2/R6 Wk-Nr 13517 'Black 11' of Major Vladimir Ferencina, 15(*Kroat*)./JG 52, Jelisavetinskaya, August 1942

16
Bf 109G-2 Wk-Nr 13577 'Black 1' of Oberstleutnant Franjo Dzal, CO of 15(*Kroat*)/JG 52, Jelisavetinskaya,
September 1942

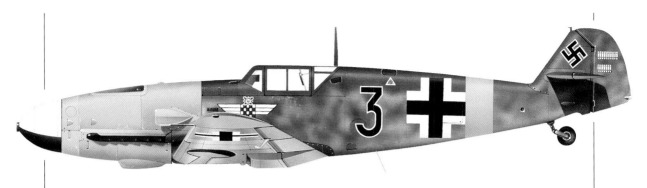

17
Bf 109G-2 Wk-Nr 13432 'Black 3' of Oberfahnrich Cvitan Galic, 15(*Kroat*)./JG 52, Maikop, September 1942

18
Bf 109G-2 'Black 4' of Leutnant Jure Lasta, 15(*Kroat*)./JG 52, Jelisavetinskaya, October 1942

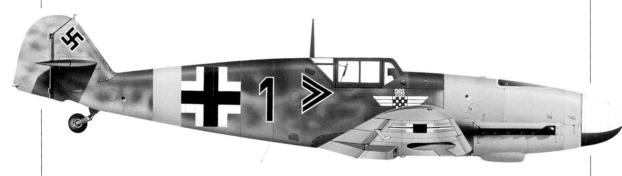

19
Bf 109G-2 Wk-Nr 13577 'Black double-chevron 1' of Oberstleutnant Franjo Dzal, CO of 15(*Kroat*)./JG 52, Maikop, October 1942

20
Bf 109G-2 'Yellow 6' of Leutnant Cvitan Galic, 15(*Kroat*)/JG 52, Kertch IV, May 1943

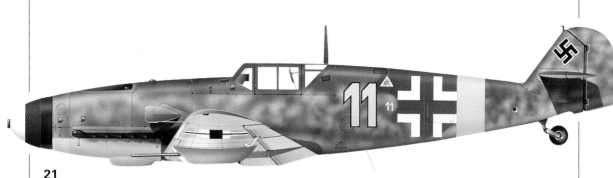

21
Bf 109G-2/R6 'Yellow 11' of Oberleutnant Albin Starc, 15(*Kroat*)./JG 52, Gukovo, May 1943

22
Bf 109G-2 'Yellow 12' of Oberleutnant Ljudevit Bencetic, 15(*Kroat*)./JG 52, Taman, May 1943

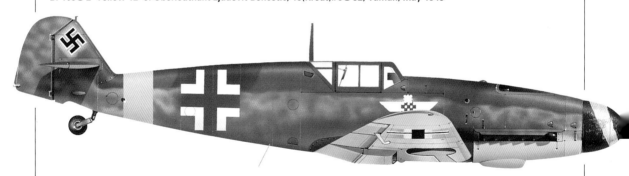

23
Bf 109G-4 of Unteroffizier Vladimir Kres, 15(*Kroat*)./JG 52, Karankut, November 1943

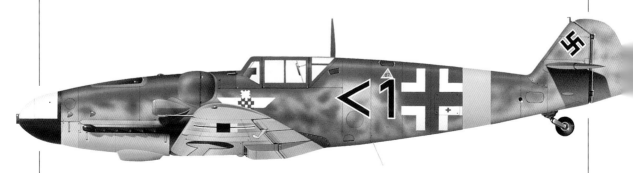

24
Bf 109G-6 'Black chevron 1' of Oberleutnant Mato Dukovac, CO of 15(*Kroat*)./JG 52, Kertch, November 1943

25
Bf 109G-6 Wk-Nr 18497 'White 13' of Unteroffizier Zdenko Avdic, 15(*Kroat*)./JG 52, Kertch, November 1943

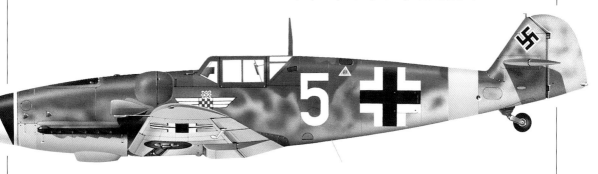

26
Bf 109G-6 'White 5' of Unteroffizier Josip Kranjc, 15(*Kroat*)./JG 52, Karankut, November 1944

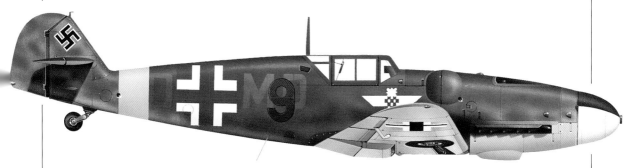

27
Bf 109G-6 Wk-Nr 19680 'Red 9' of Unteroffizier Eduard Martinko, 15(*Kroat*)./JG 52, Kertch, November 1943

28
G.50bis '3504' of por Tomislav Kauzlaric, 21.Lovacko Jato, Borongaj, April 1944

29
C.202 'Black 1' of Hauptmann Josip Helebrant, CO of 2/JGr *Kro*, Pleso, May 1944

30
MS 406c '2323' of sat Ljudevit Bencetic, CO of 14.ZJ, Zaluzani, September 1944

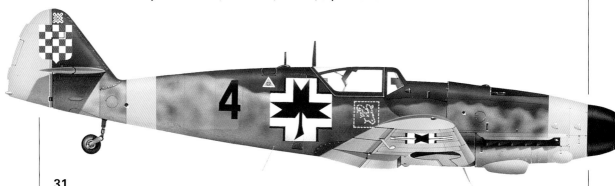

31
Bf 109G-10 'Black 4' (2104) of Boj Zlatko Stipcic, 2.LJ, Lucko, March 1945

32

Yak-3 'Yellow 12' of kap Miljenko Lipovscak, CO of 113. Lovacki Puk, Pleso, May 1945

THE SECOND COMBAT TOUR

The men of 15(*Kroatische*)./JG 52 did not enjoy a particularly long rest from operational flying, for they commenced their return journey from Zagreb to the Eastern Front on 12 February 1943. Eleven Bf 109G-2s were collected at Krakow, in Poland, en route, and just after midday on 18 February four *Gustavs* took-off in bad weather for Lvov, followed by seven more ten minutes later.

Of the first group to depart, only the experienced Major Ferencina completed the journey. Leutnante Antic and Vice force-landed six miles(ten kilometres) short of their destination and Oberfeldwebel Josip Cipic was killed in an attempted crash-landing in Bf 109G-2 'KJ+GB' 25 miles (40 km) north of Lvov. The second group, however, enjoyed better luck. After stopping at Krosno, Hauptleute Stipcic and Helebrant, Oberleutnant Bencetic, Leutnante Galic and Dukovac and Feldwebeln Mihelcic and Bartulovic arrived at Lvov.

On the 21st, deputy CO Ferencina pressed on with six pilots to Nikolayev, leaving Bencetic to rejoin the unit on 4 March. Feldwebel Mihelcic was also forced to stay behind at Uman (one of the intermediate stops on the route) until 13 March.

During the unit's absence from the frontline, the *Wehrmacht*'s situation had changed dramatically. After the defeat at Stalingrad (where many Croat infantry legionnaires also lost their lives), the strategic initiative had passed to the Red Army. In the Caucasus, 1. *Panzer Armee* and 17. *Armee* were in retreat, and by the end of April they had established a defensive line in the Kuban valley. By now the frontline stretched from Novorossiysk to Krimsk, Krasniy Oktyabr and Temryuk.

Conditions in the air had also changed. After suffering terrible losses in 1941–42, Soviet pilots were now gaining confidence. They were flying better aircraft, many of which had been supplied from the US and Britain, and had learned a lot about tactics. But, in general, Luftwaffe fighter pilots retained their edge in terms of their training and aircraft performance. Now, the primary objective of *VIII Fliegerkorps* was to give maximum protection to the retreating army. Opposing it were the 4th and 5th Soviet Air Armies.

On 30 March, 15(*Kroat*)./JG 52 moved from Nikolayev to Kertch

From left to right, Major Ferencina, Oberstleutnant Dzal and Leutnant Ivanic are seen at Taman in March 1943, having just arrived back on the Eastern Front from Croatia. The legionnaires soon found that many things had changed during their brief three-month absence (*S Ostric*)

IV airfield. Its first missions over the front were flown the following day, but the unit did not get off to a good start. Whilst on a *Freie Jagd* near Slavjanskaya, Leutnante Cvitan Galic and Andjelko Antic tangled with eight LaGG-3s, and the inexperienced Antic got separated from his leader. Galic last saw his wingman's Bf 109G-2 ('White 10' Wk-Nr 14824) trailing white smoke before it crashed.

The first claim of the unit's second tour was made on 1 April. While on a *Freie Jagd* sweep of the Novorossiysk–Slavjanskaya–Petrovskaya area, four *Gustavs* attacked eight LaGG-3s, and Galic, in 'Yellow 6', claimed one over Russahoff. The next day the unit moved to Taman, and on the 7th Franjo Dzal, returning from Croatia in the unit's Bf 108B hack ('BD+JG'), overshot the runway at Anapa and crashed, suffering slight injuries in the process.

On the 11th, a *Rotte* comprising Galic and Mihelcic engaged numerous *Ratas*, MiGs and LaGGs between Abinskaya and Megrelyskoye – Mihelcic claimed an I-16. Later that day Leutnant Nikola Vice was injured when his Bf 109G-2 (Wk-Nr 13630) crashed on take-off.

During the afternoon of 15 April, Dukovac and Mihelcic took off on a *Freie Jagd* of the Krimskaja-Abinskaja area. Dukovac subsequently related the mission details to a Croatian war correspondent:

'We reached the first battle lines at 11,400 ft (3500 m). We were careful because I know well that whoever attacks first, surprising the enemy, wins the battle. The sky was

The sleeping quarters for 15(*Kroat*)./JG 52's personnel at Kertch were somewhat on the austere side to say the least! Is it any wonder that the legionnaires suffered from all kinds of illnesses and diseases (*S Osric*)

Ferencina, Galic, Dzal and an unknown Luftwaffe officer share a joke at Taman in the spring of 1943. Note the Fi 156 Storch in the background (*S Ostric*)

Mato Dukovac (second from left) explains how he shot down an Airacobra whilst unwrapping his celebratory bottle of brandy. With the heavy drinkers in his *Staffel*, this wasn't going to last for long! The others are, from left to right, Mihelcic, Bencetic, Helebrant, Vice, Dzal, Ferencina, Galic and an unknown mechanic (*S Ostric*)

clear, with a few clouds here and there, but no trace of the enemy. We'd been in the air for half an hour, and I began to lose hope of finding the enemy. Then, suddenly, I saw four almost invisible dots in the far distance to starboard. At that moment I was overwhelmed by excitement, by some kind of fever. I immediately warned my wingman over the radio of what I had seen.

'Making a sharp turn, we started to close on the dots. I was quite happy when I saw red stars on them. It seemed the enemy had seen us too, as they quickly gained height. The battle for life and death – the battle for height – had begun. Thanks to our superior aircraft, we quickly climbed above them. Once at an altitude in excess of 16,000 ft (6,000 m) I attacked the nearest enemy, telling Viktor to follow me. It looked as if his friends had told him that I was on his tail. He tried to shake me off with various manoeuvres, but I followed every step and waited for the opportunity to open fire.

'When I closed to 165ft (50 m), I had him in the middle of my gun sight. I pressed the button and fired a short burst from all my guns. I saw by the tracers that my aim was good. He streamed blue vapour and started to dive over his territory. I still had him in my sights, and I fired one more short burst, then a small flame appeared. I fired again and he flamed like a torch, before abruptly falling away. I immediately turned to starboard and flew close to the diving fighter. I was surprised to see that it was an American-made Airacobra, a type that had only recently appeared in our sector of the front.'

On 20 April, Dukovac was delayed in his take-off by five minutes, which meant that when he claimed one of the four LaGG-3s he subsequently engaged there were no witnesses from his *Schwarm* to allow his victory to be credited to him.

Dukovac again sortied that afternoon, along with Galic, Mihelcic and Bartulovic. The Croats were escorting Ju 87s and Ju 88s to Novorossiysk when they encountered 25 Soviet fighters and flying boats over the Black Sea. Galic claimed a Chyetverikov MDR-6 flying boat, and five minutes later Dukovac downed a LaGG-3. Frustratingly for him, his second success of the day again went unnoticed. Dukovac's victim was possibly one of two 269.IAP aircraft lost in that area during the day. Upon returning to base, Mihelcic belly-landed when his landing gear failed to lower.

The following day Dukovac and Galic went out on a morning *Freie Jagd* and encountered six MiG-3s near Kabardinovka. Dukovac claimed one but Galic's 'Yellow 6' was hit and they had to withdraw. During an aternoon mission, Dukovac and Bartulovic fought numerous LaGG-3s between Novorossiysk and Gelendzhik, Dukovac claiming two (one of which was not witnessed) and Bartulovic a third. Their aircraft recognition may, however, have been at fault, as the day's only known LaGG-3 losses were three 267.IAP machines downed that morning.

On the morning of 22 April, after attacking shipping in Novorossiysk harbour, Dukovac force-landed his Bf 109G-2 (Wk-Nr 13761, which in November 1943 was sold to Finland, where it was coded MT-236) when it suffered engine trouble. He sortied again in another *Gustav* later that same day as wingman to Galic, and during this mission the pair engaged numerous enemy aircraft over the Black Sea. Galic ('Yellow 6') shot down an MDR-6, and five minutes later Dukovac ('Black 7') got a DB-3.

Pilots of 15.*Staffel* relax beside 'Yellow 6' in early May 1943. They are, from left to right, Bozidar Bartulovic, Josip Helebrant, Vladimir Ferencina, Franjo Dzal, Cvitan Galic, Nikola Vice, Mato Dukovac, Viktor Mihelcic and Ljudevit Bencetic (*J Novak*)

An early morning mission on the 25th saw Galic, Bartulovic ('Yellow 14'), Vice ('White 14') and Dukovac tasked with escorting Hs 129s and Fw 190s that had been sent to attack shipping near the vallage of Primorsko Ahtirskaya. The Croat pilots also got in on the action, helping to sink two small vessels. Returning to the target area that afternoon with the Hs 129s, Vice and Mihelcic spotted a pair of camouflaged biplanes on the ground and duly strafed them until they both burst into flames.

Galic ('Yellow 6') and Dukovac ('White 14') enjoyed yet more success two days later when they shot down two intercepting LaGG-3s between Krimskaya and Abinskaya whilst escorting He 111s. Bartulovic ('Yellow 14') got a third LaGG fighter a few minutes later.

On the final day of April, Galic and Dukovac tangled with more LaGG-3s whilst on a *Freie Jagd* sweep. Becoming separated during the engagement, Dukovac went on to down a fighter east of Jelisavetinskaya, but his success went unobserved by Galic.

By the beginning of May 1943, German troops were successfully holding defensive positions which ran through Leningrad, Smolensk, Rilsk, Harkov and Taganrog, and ended at the Sea of Asov. The Red Army's efforts to make a breakthrough in this area met with strong resistance, and the Germans extracted a heavy price for any gains made by the communists. Soviet reserves were immense, however, and more and more aircraft, tanks and soldiers were now being thrown into the battle.

On 1 May Leutnant Dukovac sank a small vessel, and the next day he was joined by Helebrant, Galic and Mihelcic on an escort mission for a formation of Luftwaffe He 111s. Two LaGG-3s tried to intercept the bombers, and both were claimed as destroyed, although unwitnessed, by Galic in his usual 'Yellow 6' and by Dukovac in 'Black 9'.

3 May proved to be a good day for the Croat pilots, who claimed five Soviet aircraft destroyed. Dukovac was again the first to score, claiming one of four LaGG-3s encountered by the unit at 0830 hrs near Krimskaya

– Soviet sources list no LaGGs lost in this battle, however. The day's next mission was flown by Galic (in 'Yellow 6') and Mihelcic, and it proved to be yet another eventful one. Firstly, they fought an inconclusive battle with three 57.GIAP Spitfires and two LaGG-3s, during which Mihelcic's starboard wing was hit by cannon fire. Five minutes later they encountered a large formation of 14 DB-3s, seven Il-2s and Il-2M3s and 16 fighters. In the brief engagement that followed, Galic claimed an Il-2M3 and Mihelcic an Il-2.

During the afternoon, while escorting *Panzerjäger* Hs 129s, Galic and Dukovac intercepted seven Il-2s and six fighters near Novobahanskoye. Galic claimed one of the fighters and Dukovac an Il-2, although the former's 'Yellow 6' was damaged and he had to force-land upon his return to Taman airfield.

On 4 May another 15(*Kroat*)./JG 52 pilot failed to return from a mission. Three Bf 109Gs had sortied at 0820 hrs as escorts for He 111s, but Bencetic had been forced to return early due to engine trouble and Dukovac force-landed near Varenikovskaya. Oberfeldwebel Mihelcic was believed to have skirmished with Soviet fighters, but neither he nor his Bf 109G-2 ('Yellow 9' Wk-Nr 13516) were heard of again. That day the Red Army regained control of Krimskaya.

5 May saw Dukovac and Bartulovic attack seven LaGG-3s near Krimskaya, each pilot claiming two kills. During the evening's Stuka escort mission, Dukovac downed his third victory of the day – another LaGG.

Both men excelled once more on the 6th. On the first mission of the day, Bencetic and Bartulovic were attacked by a mixed fighter formation as they escorted Ju 88s, and the latter pilot succeeded in destroying two LaGG-3s within the space of ten minutes. Bencetic ('Yellow 12') claimed a Yak-1. That evening another Stuka escort was flown, and during the course of the mission the inevitable encounter with LaGG-3s occurred and Dukovac and Bartulovic each claimed a fighter destroyed.

On 8 May, while escorting an Fi 156 Storch, Dukovac, in 'Black 2', claimed a LaGG 3 at 1115 hrs. Two minutes later, his wingman, Bozidar Bartulovic, also downed a LaGG-3, which would prove to be his last Eastern Front kill. Soviet records state that only one LaGG was lost during the day, by 926.IAP, time and location unknown.

New pilots arrived at Taman on 12 May, namely ex-VVKJ fighter pilots Hauptleute Bogdan Vujicic and Nikola Cvikic and Stabsfeldwebel Zivko Dzal. All three had been sent to 2./*Ergänzungsgruppe Ost* at La Rochelle, in France, in February 1943, and duly returned to Croatia in late March to await posting. When the movement orders arrived, they were joined by some 'old hands' from the previous year's battles – Oberleutnant Starc, Leutnante Boskic and Kauzlaric, Stabsfeldwebel Martinasevic and Unteroffizier Misic. After a handful of familiarisation flights, all except Kauzlaric were considered combat-ready.

On 13 May, Galic had a narrow escape when his Bf 109G-2 (Wk-Nr

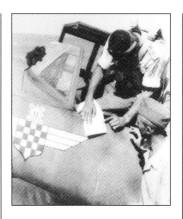

Oberfeldwebel Viktor Mihelcic makes a last-minute check of his map before departing on yet another mission in the early spring of 1943. Having two victories to his credit, the Slovene was lost on 4 May 1943 when he was overwhelmed by a superior force of Soviet fighters (*S Ostric*)

Bf 109G-2 'Yellow 12' of 15(*Kroat*)./JG 52 is prepared for its next sortie out in the open at Kertch in the spring of 1943. Fifteen-kill ace Ljudevit Bencetic claimed a Yak-1 whilst flying this aircraft on 6 May 1943 (*S Ostric*)

Engine covers hinged open, an unidentified *Gustav* of 15(*Kroat*)./ JG 52 awaits attention from hard-pressed groundcrews at Taman in the spring of 1943. Note the 'Croat spinner', the first segment of which was white, the second red and the third black/green (RLM 70) (*S Ostric*)

Oberstleutnant Dzal (hand in the air) and Major Ferencina (obscured by Dzal) seem more interested in the *Staffel* dog than in receiving reports from Leutnant Vice and Feldwebel Bartulovic, both of whom are standing to attention at the salute! (*S Ostric*)

13642) was written off in a crash on landing due to a faulty tyre. Two days later Oberstleutnant Dzal made his only operational sortie of this period when he personally led his younger brother Zivko on his debut mission. Together with Galic and Dukovac, they flew an uneventful Ju 88 escort mission.

A week later Dzal found himself in command of the whole HZL. In preparation for expansion, Major Ferencina was appointed CO of 10.ZLJ, and 11.ZLJ was re-established under Stipcic. Dzal's place at the head of 4.ZLS was given to an inexperienced, but 'reliable', fighter pilot in Major Ivan Cenic, who was then completing his training with JG 104.

On 24 May, Hauptmann Cvikic force-landed in a field about nine miles (15 km) east of Taman after the engine in his Bf 109G-1 (Wk-Nr 14032) caught fire, while Leutnant Boskic damaged his *Gustav* during a one-wheel landing at Taman.

The next day a *Schwarm* escorting a *Gruppe* of Stukas was attacked by four Spitfires Vs of 57.GIAP south-east of Temryuk. Two of the Soviet fighters were claimed by Dukovac in 'Black 7' and another by Galic in 'Yellow 6'. The only possible match for these claims in Soviet records, however, is one Spitfire, which crash-landed at 1645 hrs near Svistelnikovo, reputedly after a clash with an Fw 190. For the second day running Cvikic force-landed, although this time his fighter had received combat damage.

The two units clashed again on 26 May, and although the first two encounters were inconclusive, in the third engagement Bencetic claimed to have forced a Spitfire down north-west of Krimskaya after four *Gustavs* met 15 Spitfires, LaGGs and *Stormoviks* while escorting Ju 87s.

During a *Freie Jagd* sweep on the 27th, Cvikic ('Black 8'), Galic ('Yellow 6') and Dukovac surprised eight LaGG-3s west of Trarehof. Each pilot claimed one of the Soviet fighters destroyed, although Dukovac's kill was not witnessed by his comrades. On the 30th he downed yet another LaGG while escorting 40 He 111s attacking Krasnodar. This proved to be the unit's final victory for the month. That same day, the still unfit Oberfahnrich Tomislav Kauzlaric was sent back home.

The beginning of June found the Red Air Force licking its wounds after sustaining big losses (more than 2,000 aircraft destroyed according to German sources) in the aerial battles fought over Kuban. Operations were significantly reduced over the southern front, but there were still occasional clashes such as when, on 5 June, five aircraft on a *Freie Jagd* sweep of the

Krimskaya area found a pair of LaGG-3s. Galic shot down both of them, although his second victory remained unconfirmed.

The following day, Galic ('Yellow 6') and Stabsfeldwebel Zivko Dzal ('Yellow 1') were performing escort duty over the Black Sea when two Pe-2s, four Il-2/M3s and six Yak-1s appeared. During the course of the engagement the CO's brother claimed his sole victory when he downed a Yak-1. Of greater significance, though, was the fact that this victory represented the unit's 200th confirmed kill, although this figure does not include unconfirmed victories that were later upgraded.

That same afternoon, Galic was escorting a reconnaissance *Gustav* of NAGr 9, sent to photograph Soviet artillery positions, when he was able to add another LaGG-3 to the scoreboard.

During the night of 9/10 June, Stabsfeldwebel Ivan Sekeres, who regularly flew the unit's hack Klemm 35, was killed during a Po 2 raid.

DESERTIONS

It was during this second tour that cracks started to appear in the loyalty of Croat fighter pilots towards the Luftwaffe. In April 1943 eight former VVKJ fighter pilots sent to 2./*Ergänzungsgruppe Ost* at La Rochelle deliberately failed their medicals. The remaining four, Majors Ivan Cenic and Juraj Jankovski, Hauptmann Arsenije Ikonjikov and Leutnant Karlo Sencic, were sent for JG 104 for further training.

Then, on 14 May, Albin Starc and Bogdan Vujicic failed to return in their Bf 109G-2s ('Yellow 11' Wk-Nr 14545 and 'White 2' Wk-Nr 13485, respectively) from a *Freie Jagd* sweep of the Krimskaya area. They radioed that they were engaging fighters, but they had actually landed at the Soviet-held airfield at Byelaya Glina, north-east of Krasnodar.

Both men had been planning their defection for some time, and Starc had been in contact with communist activists within the ZNDH soon after his return to Croatia the previous winter. He had even been given a password to ensure his safe reception by the Soviets when the time came.

Vujicic was also a communist sympathiser, but he had additional reasons for his change of loyalty. A Serb, his family had died in *Ustasa* mass murders in 1941. He had been imprisoned and was awaiting execution when a pre war Military Academy classmate, Vladimir Kren (who now happened to be ZNDH C in C), learned of his predicament and sought his friend's release. Freed on condition that he changed his religion from Orthodox to Catholic, his acceptance by the ZNDH, and later the HZL, was arranged by his friend. Vujicic completed one tour as CO of the HZL bomber element, 15(*Kroat*)./KG 53, before transferring to fighters.

It did not take the Germans long to discover the truth behind the disappearances, although the Croatian high command refused to believe it, and even had the names of both men inscribed on a memorial plate erected in Zagreb.

Bogdan Vujicic, Vladimir Ferencina and Nikola Cvikic photographed together the day before Vujicic's defection to the Soviets on 14 May 1943. Cvikic would follow him one month later (*S Ostric*)

A further defection came on 15 June after Cvikic, Dukovac, Galic and Martinasevic were scrambled. Cvikic returned five minutes later, complaining about propeller-pitch malfunction on his Bf 109G-2 'Yellow 2' (Wk-Nr 14205). He took off again but did not return. Like Starc and Vujicic, he had landed at Byelaya. A Croatian Serb, Nikola Cvikic had renounced his Orthodox religion to become a Catholic, which was the only way Serbs could remain in the NDH. He was later to serve with distinction in the post war Yugoslav Air Force.

This spate of defections enraged the Germans, and the RLM immediately grounded the remaining Croat pilots and urgently summoned Oberstleutnant Dzal to Simferopol for questioning. The unit was then withdrawn from the front, and by 20 June only ten more sorties by 'reliable' pilots had been made. General Kren dismissed Franjo Dzal from command of HZL, replacing him with Oberstleutnant Pavao Sic.

But there were was still one more defection to come. On 20 July, while on a courier flight from Simferopol to Nikolayev, Leutnant Nikola Vice and groundcrewman Stabsfeldwebel Josip Usljebrk escaped across the Black Sea to Turkey in Klemm Kl 35 'CI+SF' Wk-Nr 3279.

Apart from the defections, losses during the second tour had amounted to four pilots dead, but in less than three months 15(*Kroatische*)./JG 52 had claimed 37 confirmed and nine unconfirmed aerial victories (five of which were later confirmed), plus two aircraft destroyed on the ground. The majority of these victories were credited to three pilots – Bozidar Bartulovic (eight), Cvitan Galic (ten, plus two unconfirmed) and Mato Dukovac (14 and six unconfirmed, five of which were subsequently upgraded). Dukovac had distinguished himself most of all, with hardly a day passing without him demonstrating his marksmanship and, indeed, all the natural skills of the fighter pilot.

Apart from Galic, most of the veterans from 1941–42 seemed more interested in survival than in adding to their scores. After Stalingrad, it had become increasingly obvious that the Axis was not winning the war. Franjo Dzal sought solace in drink and was rarely sober – he flew just one sortie. His deputy, Vladimir Ferencina, flew 16 missions during April and then stopped. Zlatko Stipcic was confined to staff duties, and flew only occasional courier trips in the unit's Kl 35 and Bf 108. Josip Helebrant flew 33 sorties and participated in some inconclusive air battles, while Ljudevit Bencetic completed 35 sorties and claimed one confirmed victory and one unconfirmed. Safet Boskic and Stjepan Martinasevic, who rejoined the unit in early 1943, completed 46 and 44 missions respectively during a month of flying, yet failed to add to their scores.

The RLM considered these men (branded 'Yugos' by the Germans) to be either too old or too unreliable for further operations, and none went back to the front. The unit did fight again, but only after an infusion of younger men who were then still in training in Germany.

Hauptmann Cvikic, Leutnante Dukovac and Galic and Oberleutnant Bencetic are debriefed by ZNDH CO Vladimir Kren, under the watchful eye of Oberstleutnant Dzal, in late April 1943 (*J Novak*)

SAME TASKS, NEW MEN

During the summer of 1941 the ZNDH had announced that it was seeking to recruit men for training as pilots. There were many applicants, and the 40 candidates selected assembled at Borongaj airfield in September to start training the following month with 1. *Docastnicko Popunidbeno Jato* (DPJ – NCO Training Squadron). This unit formed the Croatian element of the Luftwaffe's *Flugzeugführerschüle* A/B 123.

One year later the remaining pupils joined the Luftwaffe's A/B 123 proper, and by 8 March 1943 they had completed basic pilot training. Twenty-one candidates were then sent to JG 104 at Fürth, where

Instructors (sitting) and cadets of 1.DPJ pose for a course photograph at Borongaj airfield in January 1942. Five members of 1.DPJ – Martinko, Avdic, Kranjc, Gazapi and Kres – subsequently became aces with 15(*Kroat*)./JG 52 (*Authors*)

Accidents were not uncommon during training. This minor incident, in the autumn of 1942, saw student Ferdo Gilderman wipe the fixed undercarriage off an unfortunate Gotha Go 145 (*Authors*)

51

they started the fighter pilot's course, which ran from 1 April until 15 September. In mid-July they were joined by some of the most experienced Croat legionnaires, who shared with them their knowledge and experience of aerial fighting.

Twelve students graduated on 1 October, and they were destined to serve with 15(*Kroatische*)./JG 52 during its third tour on the Eastern Front. Here, they were joined by 2.DPJ pilots Skarda and Martan,

who had started their training a little later, but were nevertheless considered ready for combat.

On 21 October, new *Staffelkapitan* Mato Dukovac, who had recently been promoted to oberleutnant, arrived at Nikolayev with his men – Feldwebeln Eduard Martinko and Desimir Furtinovic, and Unteroffiziere Zdenko Avdic, Josip Kranjc, Dragutin Gazapi, Vladimir Kres, Ivan Baltic, Albin Sval, Vladimir Salomon, Josip Jelacic, Zvonimir Rajteric, Ivan Sirola, Borislav Skarda and Djuro Martan. They were assigned eight Bf 109G-4s and G-6s and moved to Bagerovo, on the eastern tip of the Kertch peninsula. From there they flew their first sorties on the 26th.

It was not a promising start. On 29 October Dukovac opened the scoring by downing one of three LaGG-3s engaged south of Kertch, the Soviet fighter crashing into the sea. However, that same day the unit suffered its first loss of the tour when Unteroffizier Zvonko Rajteric died after his Bf 109G-4 (Wk-Nr 19494) stalled and crashed on take-off. The next day Dukovac added a *Stormovik* and a LaGG-3 to his tally.

On the last day of October, Gazapi claimed his first kill (a LaGG-3), which fell in the sea in sight of Bagerovo airfield. A little later, three *Stormoviks* were reported attacking Kertch, so Dukovac took off on his own and engaged them just as they were breaking off their attack. Later, he recounted the engagement to a war-correspondent:

'I selected the last aircraft in the formation and closed on him. The gunner saw me and wildly opened fire, but it was too late – I was so close

that his own tail protected me. His friends seemed unaware of what was going on around them. I aimed, pressed the trigger and fired a few shots. The gunner was silenced. I fired once more and he burst into flames and dived towards the ground. I was happy with my victory – but not for long.

'It seemed that the remaining two pilots had seen their friend's fate and they dived after me, firing as they closed in on my fighter. I thought that I was done for, but their aim was poor. A torrent of bullets passed

Unteroffizier Vladimir Kres (left) and his CO, 44-kill ace Oberleutnant Mato Dukovac (right), are seen at the completion of yet another mission in November 1943. Kres claimed eight victories (six of them confirmed), and by 11 March 1944 he was 15 (*Kroat*)./JG 52's only combat-fit pilot. All the others had either been killed or hospitalised (*Authors*)

The first casualty of 15 (*Kroat*)./JG 52's third tour was Unteroffizier Zvonimir Rajteric, who was killed when his Bf 109G-4 (Wk-Nr 19494) overturned whilst attempting to take off from Bagerovo airfield on 29 October 1943. This veteran fighter had previously been operated by 13(*Slowak*)./JG 52 (*J Novak*)

over, under and either side of me. I wanted to attack again but I was only just above the sea.'

Dukovac's victim crashed into the sea south of Kertch, and in sight of a *Wehrmacht* observation post.

1 November 1943 proved to be HZL's most successful day on the Russian Front. Whilst flying his first ever combat sortie, Eduard Martinko claimed a Pe-2 at first light. Ten minutes later Mato Dukovac downed an Il-2M3 south of Kertch, then, in combat with seven Airacobras, Dragutin Gazapi destroyed one of them. A little later Josip Kranjc claimed a LaGG-3, followed shortly afterwards by Martinko, who this time 'bagged' an Il-2. Gazapi got another LaGG-3, and in the afternoon a third Il-2 fell to Martinko, while his wingman Vladimir Salomon was credited with a LaGG 3. Before the hour was out Dukovac claimed a fourth Il-2 and Zdenko Avdic a fifth. Finally, Eduard Martinko enjoyed the distinction of downing the last kill of the day when he destroyed an Airacobra, taking his personal score to four kills in just a matter of hours, and boosting 15(*Kroatische*)./JG 52's 1 November haul to 11.

The following afternoon, Dukovac intercepted three *Stormoviks* over Bagerovo airfield and shot one of them down. Gazapi, meanwhile, engaged four Il-2M3s while escorting German bombers over Kertch and succeeded in destroying one of them. His Bf 109G-4 (Wk-Nr 19543) was then hit by escorting Airacobras, and he was forced to crash-land at Bagerovo.

That same day Martinko claimed an 'ancient' I-153 *Chaika* to 'make ace'. All five of his kills had been scored in his first 48 hours in combat. At the same time, south of Kertch, Dukovac engaged seven Il-2M3s and three Airacobras. Having quickly claimed a *Stormovik*, the Croat was set upon by the trio of US-built fighters, and his aircraft was riddled with bullets. Crash-landing near Mariental, Dukovac escaped uninjured, but his Bf 109G-4 (Wk-Nr 1497513, which had previously been operated by *Slovakische*./JG 52, and flown by top Slovak ace Jan Reznák) was wrecked.

Also enjoying success on this day was Zdenko Avdic, who claimed two LaGG-3s, and Josip Kranjc, who claimed a third LaGG.

The day was noteworthy for another reason too, as the Luftwaffe's supreme commander, *Reichsmarschall* Hermann Göring, issued an order which stated that 'Oberstleutnant Franjo Dzal is to take command of HZL at once, in the position of *Geschwaderkommodore*'.

On 6 November, Gazapi and Baltic each claimed a LaGG-3 over Mariental, but the next day Unteroffizier Vladimir Salomon was forced to bail out of his Bf 109G-6 (Wk-Nr 20039) after clashing with Airacobras and La-5s over the Sea of Azov. Although he came down little more than one mile (two kilometres) from the shore, he died within minutes in the freezing water. And on the 12th there was a narrow escape for Martinko when German flak hit his Bf 109G-6 ('Red 9' Wk-Nr 19680), and he crash-landed four miles (six kilometres) from Kertch. Dukovac had, however, sent a DB-3 crashing into the sea after clashing with eight fighters and five bombers during the same sortie.

There was more success for the Croats the next day when, during an early morning patrol east of Kertch, Avdic and Kranjc claimed two fighters apiece. Two hours later, Martinko claimed two LaGG-3s and

Gazapi a third from the five they intercepted over Kertch. At about the same time, Avdic and Kranjc had been attacked by four fighters while escorting an Fw 189. Kranjc shot down two and Avdic one. All these victories were confirmed by the Fw 189's crew. Their 'bag' for the day totalled seven Soviet fighters – a LaGG-3, Yak-1, La-5 and an Airacobra for Kranjc, and an La-5, Yak-1 and an Airacobra for Avdic. The next day the pair accounted for two more Airacobras over the Sea of Azov while they were escorting Ju 87s.

The unit moved to Karankut airfield on the 15th, and four days later Dukovac and Avdic each managed to down a LaGG-3. On 21 November, whilst flying Bf 109G-6 'White 13' (Wk-Nr 18497), Zdenko Avdic's brief frontline career was prematurely cut short, as he explains in the following account:

'We were escorting Stukas when two LaGG-3s tried to attack. Dukovac quickly despatched the first one and I went after the second. I approached it with the sun at my back and attacked from underneath. The LaGG went into a spin and crashed. Despite our fuel now being on the low side, Dukovac decided to stay over the front a little longer.

'At that moment I saw four LaGGs rapidly approaching us from behind. Our evasive manoeuvre in these circumstances was always to pull back on the stick so as to take advantage of the *Gustav*'s superior rate of climb. To counter such tactics, the Russians always kept pairs of aircraft above us, stepped up at intervals of 3000 ft (1000 m).

'Suddenly, there was a dreadful explosion in the cockpit and I felt a terrible pain in my left arm. I just dived into the abyss. I tried to check my speed, but my arm didn't obey. To my horror, I saw my hand was separated from the rest of my arm, the fingers still around the throttle. I had to move them. Holding the stick with my legs, I used all the strength of my other hand. The bleeding was immense, and I felt my eyes grow dark. More by instinct I let the *Gustav* fly itself. It glided down and landed five miles (eight kilometres) inside our territory. German grenadiers came and took me to a field hospital.'

Unteroffizier Dragutin Gazapi was not so lucky when he crashed in flames in his Bf 109G-6 (Wk-Nr 19475) on 27 November after being attacked by an Airacobra. The P-39s drew blood again the next day when Unteroffizier Kres forced-landed his damaged Bf 109G-4 (Wk-Nr 19208) at Karankut airfield.

The weather closed in at the end of November, and virtually all flying was curtailed until February 1944. Occasional sorties where mounted during December and January, but there were few successes to avenge these losses. On 6 December, Dukovac claimed two *Stormoviks* near Bagerovo for his 30th and 31st confirmed kills.

On 21 December, two more Croatians were shot down, including Unteroffizier Ivan Baltic, who recounts what happened that day;

Unteroffizier Kres forced-landed after combat with Soviet Airacobras on 28 November 1943. Most HZL veterans considered the Airacobra to be their toughest adversary on the Eastern Front (*J Novak*)

'I was flying with Kranjc when countless Airacobras attacked us. There was no way out – we had to fight. I lost sight of Kranjc. The Russians were all around. I had flown 36 sorties and scored four victories, but the odds had never been so bad. Now, an Airacobra faced me. We flew head-on and both of us fired, but I lost my nerve and broke upwards. Then he hit me. I saw him zoom past with his engine smoking. My aircraft started to tremble and smoke. I was too low to bail out so I crash-landed in a field near Kertch. It was a rough landing and the aircraft overturned, seriously injuring my back. Long treatment awaited me. Anyway, it was the end of my flying in Russia. I claimed hits on my opponent, but because I didn't see him crash I got an unconfirmed kill. Later I heard that Kranjc had been killed.'

Actually, Unterofficizier Josip Kranjc had managed to escape unharmed. But luck deserted him on his next sortie. He and Vladimir Kres flew a weather-reconnaissance mission in extreme conditions, and with his fuel getting low, Kranjc dived into cloud to make visual contact with the ground and establish their position. He misjudged his height, however, and flew straight into the ground near Perekop.

At the beginning of January 1944, 12-kill ace Feldwebel Eduard Martinko crashed a Bf 109G during a ferry flight near Uman and was seriously injured. The first victory of the new year was achieved by Dukovac on 12 January when he claimed a Yak-1. Then, on the 24th, Kres claimed an Airacobra, and Jelacic destroyed a LaGG-3 the following day. Kres and Sval enjoyed more success on the 28th when each of them claimed a LaGG-3, and they repeated this feat on 10 February.

The unit was struck a serious blow 15 days later when it temporarily lost its CO, the high-scoring Mato Dukovac. During his first sortie of the day, he and his wingman, Kres, had each claimed a Yak-1. On their second mission they had encountered two Yak-9s and an Airacobra, and after downing one of the Yaks, Dukovac also despatched the P-39. His wingman had, in the meantime, claimed the second Yak. Then, on his fifth mission of the day, Dukovac was shot down by Airacobras, crash-landing near Bagerovo. He injured his back and spine upon hitting the ground at high speed, the impact writing off his Bf 109G-6 ('Black 1').

Dukovac was sent to a German field hospital, and after surviving a night nuisance raid by Po 2s, he returned to this unit at Karankut as soon as he could walk some days later. By then the *Staffel* had been decimated, and only three pilots remained fit for duty

Things got worse on 10 March when Unteroffizier Albin Sval crashed and was killed during a seemingly routine test flight near Otary . The next day the two remaining pilots flew 15(*Kroatische*)./JG 52's final combat mission of the war, during which Unteroffizier Vladimir Kres claimed an Airacobra. It was the unit's 285th confirmed kill, although 12 more were later added when unconfirmed victories were officially recognised.

On 12 March the unit lost yet another pilot when Feldwebel Desimir Furtinovic was taken to hospital suffering from kidney failure brought on by the low-quality drinking water. This was one of the numerous ailments (hepatitis was another) that were common among men serving in the Crimea.

Although more new pilots were expected, the RLM accepted the futility of keeping such a decimated outfit in the frontline. The homeward journey

for the surviving Croatian pilots and groundcrewmen began on 15 March, and by 1 April most of the unit's remaining personnel had arrived in Zagreb. A liaison detachment remained at Nikolayev, although this soon moved, firstly to Odessa and then to Zilistea.

The results of the previous five months' fighting were depressing, for although 68 confirmed and 17 unconfirmed (of which nine were later confirmed) victories had been scored, five pilots were dead, four had been seriously wounded and five were ill. Yet help was on the way.

While 15(*Kroat*)./JG 52 was fighting with the Luftwaffe in the USSR, another group of Croat fighter pilots had been in training. Back in 1941, 80 candidates had been accepted for pilot training within 2.DPJ by the Italians at Mostar. There were two batches, the first 40 starting in November and the others the following spring.

At the end of their basic training, three groups of ten, including some from 1.DPJ, were posted to JG 104, at Fürth, between 28 April and 28 June 1943. Come the end of December, Unteroffiziere Nikola Hulina, Jeronim Jankovic, Ignacije Lucin, Zvonko Mikulec, Ivan Mihaljevic, Vladimir Sandtner and

Unteroffizier Albin Sval is seen with his Bf 109G-5 'Black 5' (Wk-Nr 15770), which he had to force-land after it suffered combat damage on 25 November 1943. Sval scored three confirmed and two unconfirmed victories before being killed test-flying a *Gustav* near Otary on 10 March 1944 (*Bundesarchiv via D Bernad*)

This IMAM RO.41 fighter-trainer was operated by the Italian flying school at Mostar that was attended by 2.DPJ cadets in 1942 (*Authors*)

2.DPJ cadets and their Italian instructor (centre) pose for the camera alongside a SAIMAN 200 primary trainer at Mostar airfield in the summer of 1942 (*Authors*)

Oto Sifner were chosen to fill the thinned ranks of 15(*Kroat*)./JG 52. But before doing so, they were sent to gain further experience with II./EJG 1 at Saint-Jean-d'Angely, in France.

Under the tuition of *experten* Leutnant Friedrich Wachowiak (killed in action in July 1944, having claimed 86 victories) and Feldwebel Erich Buttner (thought to have been killed in 1945 with 23 victories to his credit), they learned how to fight and survive against the Soviets. On two occasions the students also encountered US bomber formations, although they were strictly forbidden from engaging them.

In mid-March 1944, the newly graduated pilots (bar Hulina), led by Wachowiak, departed for the Crimea. Upon their arrival at Nikolayev at the beginning of April, they found that 15(*Kroat*)./JG 52 had already been sent back to Croatia, so the pilots were absorbed into a German *Staffeln* within III./JG 52.

Tutor Friedrich Wachowiak had by then made a strong impression on the 'green' pilots, as Ignacije Lucin remembers:

'When we joined JG 52, it was time for us to leave Wachowiak. He took us to one side and told us once more to be as careful as possible, and never to take unnecessary risks. That man really taught us a lot. It's probably thanks to him that most of us survived the war.'

During May and June, the young Croats occasionally flew as wingmen to experienced *Jagdflieger*. During these sorties, Unteroffizier Vladimir Sandtner claimed an Il-2 confirmed and a Yak-9 unconfirmed, while Unteroffizier Jeronim Jankovic was credited with a second confirmed kill.

Back in Croatia, 1./JGr *Kroatien* (as 15(*Kroat*)./JG 52 had been re-designated) steadily regained its strength, and the RLM decided to

HZS fighter pilots are seen at Labjau, in Lithuania, in the summer of 1944. Fifth from left is 12-kill ace Eduard Martinko and eleventh is 13-kill ace Zlatko Stipcic (*J Novak*)

Hauptmann Mato Dukovac points out the the painting of a LaGG fighter on the gravestone of an unknown Soviet airman who had been shot down in 1941 at Besarabia. This photograph was taken in July 1944. Two months later Dukovac defected (*J Novak*)

Oberst Franjo Dzal (third from left) visits HZS personnel at Labjau in September 1944. A few days later Hauptmann Dukovac (third from right) and Leutnant Spoljar changed sides. Leutnant Svarc knew of their plan but refused to go with them, fearing reprisals against his family in Croatia (*J Novak*)

re-deploy it. At the beginning of July 1944, the newly promoted Hauptmann Dukovac and his men (Stabfeldwebel Eduard Martinko, Feldwebeln Vladimir Kres, Ivan Baltic and Josip Jelacic and Unteroffiziere Vinko Tatarevic, Asim Korhut, Josip Cekovic, Stjepan Klaric, Dragutin Kucinic, Jakob Petrovic, Leopold Hrastovcan and Dragutin Vranic) started off on a long journey.

Their first destination was Zilistea, in Rumania, where they were supposed to receive brand-new Bf 109s. Five pilots (Unteroffizier Lucin had been hospitalised in Croatia and arrived later) were attached to III./JG 52, and they turned up at the front during a major Soviet offensive. The expected aircraft never arrived, and the Croats were transferred to Piestany, in Slovakia, a few days later. There, they received the news that HZL had ceased to exist as of 21 July 1944. Instead, the *Hrvatska Zrakoplovna Skupina* (HZS – Croatian Air Force Group) had been formed, which became the *Hrvatska Zrakoplovna Izobrazbena Skupina* (HZIS – Croatian Air Force Training Group) on 26 September.

Still with no equipment, but with two new members (Leutnante Djuro Svarc and Vladimir Spoljar), the unit was ordered to move in August to Eichwalde airfield, near Königsberg in East Prussia, where it received ten Bf 109G-14s. At the beginning of September the unit moved once again, to Labjau airfield, in Lithuania, in preparation for its combat deployment.

In the meantime, Mato Dukovac put into action plans he had been making since the spring. On 20 September he and Vladimir Spoljar defected. Their action was quickly announced by the Soviets, whereupon the Germans ordered the unit's return to Eichwalde, prohibited all flying and, on 1 November, withdrew its aircraft.

Leutnant Djuro Svarc, the new CO of the HZIS fighter element, was immediately ordered to take his men to Poznan, and then to Sroda, in Poland, where they were to begin infantry training. This he did, and by the end of the year his small band of fully trained fighter pilots were grimly defending trenches between Frankfurt am Oder and Szczecin against the Red Army.

Puk Calogovic eventually deserted from the *Wehrmacht*, and with the help of the ZNDH Attaché in Berlin, he was able to return to Croatia, together with the pilots and some ground personnel. On the way, they collected six Croat pilots from JG 104 in Fürth and nine from JG 108 in Bad Vöslau.

By this time the HZIS, the most famous of Croatian Legion units, had ceased to exist. Its pilots had claimed 299 confirmed aerial victories, a figure which included those kills scored with III./JG 52. A further 42 to 46 kills remained unconfirmed, and five Soviet aircraft were also destroyed on the ground. The unit had flown in excess of 5000 Eastern Front sorties.

WAR RETURNS TO YUGOSLAVIA

As detailed in chapter one, Yugoslavian opposition to the German invasion in April 1941 had been largely ineffectual. With his hold on the country secure, Hitler was able to return to the item at the top of his agenda – the invasion of the USSR. And with the creation of the Croatian puppet state which followed the invasion, most German troops left for the Eastern Front. Their departure was the signal for the start of a terror campaign against the 2.2 million Serbs living in the country.

The Croatian regime's treatment of the Serbs rivalled the SS in terms of its systematic brutality, with whole villages being burned out and hundreds of thousands of people murdered or sent to death-camps. Even the *Wehrmacht* became upset at these activities, and at a South-East HQ commanders' conference in Belgrade on 27 August 1942, Oberst von Massenbach, Commaning Officer of *Süd-Ost Feldgendarmerie* HQ, castigated the Croat liaison officer for the 'anti-orthodox bloodthirstiness of *Ustasa* forces and the execution of 700,000 Serbs'. Perhaps, though, he betrayed his real concern when he added that 'due to such wrong Croat policy, now Germans will have to bleed'.

The campaign of terror had been planned and carried out mostly by *Ustasa* forces, with the Croatian Army playing no real part. After the initial shock of these massacres, Bosnian and Croatian Serbs started to take the fight back to the *Ustasa* in Herzegovina from early June 1941, followed by a bigger uprising a few weeks later. Resistance grew during the summer in other Serb-inhabited areas of the Croat puppet state, with uprisings in the Bosnia, Lika, Kordun and Banija areas, spreading later into Dalmatia and Slavonia.

There were two elements involved. One had arisen spontaneously for local protection and had no political affiliations, but the other, led by the communists, was better organised, and worked systematically to form a resistance movement that would spread throughout Yugoslavia.

Working together, the insurgents quickly freed areas of territory and captured large quantities of weapons. NDH officials were shocked. So too were their German and Italian overlords, who started counter action but never succeeded in crushing resistance. The primary task of the newly organized ZNDH, therefore, became the provision of air support for Croat and Axis forces in their action against the insurgents.

The Germans had found over 350 VVKJ aircraft in their area of occupation, and had requisitioned 50 (including 15 Bf 109Es, six Hurricane Is and a single Ikarus IK-3) for their needs. After repair, another 211 aircraft had been incorporated into the ZNDH by 20 July 1943.

The ZNDH differed from the rest of the Croatian Army mainly in its ethnic composition. The backbone was provided by 500 former VVKJ and PV officers, plus 1,600 NCOs. The majority of these men were

Croats, but there were also many 'catholicised' Serbs, Slovenes, Russians, Ukrainians, Bosnian Moslems and Germans. Many were forced to join the ZNDH, and most of them were not NDH supporters. Some, in fact, opposed it. Indeed, during the summer of 1941, sympathisers and members of the *Narodnooslobodilacki Pokret* (NOP – People's Liberation Movement) within the ZNDH indulged in sabotage and espionage.

The new air force received an unexpected blow at the end of June. The Germans had collected some 25 aircraft (including eight Furies, four Avia BH-33s and two IK-3s) for the ZNDH at Zemun airfield. They were separated by a wire fence from a dozen miscellaneous ex-VVKJ machines that had been earmarked for scrapping. While the German guards were catching up on the war news shortly after the launch of Operation *Barbarossa* (the invasion of the USSR), local patriots, including former VVKJ mechanics, moved the fence and all the aircraft were scrapped!

The first offensive flights against the rebels were carried out on 26 June 1941 over Herzegovina. The next day an ancient Potez Po 25 was shot down near Avtovac village. The ZNDH lost a further 15 aircraft in 1941, and entered 1942 with just 110 machines.

Its fighter forces were poorly equipped in every respect, consisting of 12 ex-VVKJ machines including four IK-2s (lacking spare parts), seven ancient BH-33Es and one Fury II. Fortunately for this ill-equipped force, there was no opposition, and some modern aircraft were later received. And while operations continued against the insurgents, the sabotage from within continued – even at the Zagreb headquarters. One group even organised the handing over of two aircraft to the partisans.

A few days later these aircraft were in action against their former owners when, on 4 June 1942, Rudolf Cajavec and his gunner Milutin Jazbec attacked Banja Luka. Their Breguet 19 was hit by groundfire, however, and they crash-landed near Kadinjani village. Cajavec committed suicide and Jazbec was captured and later shot.

Days later, in the first ZNDH fighter missions, three Rogozarski R-100 trainers were deployed as fighters to intercept the remaining aircraft – a Potez Po 25 – should it attempt to bomb Zagreb.

With Franjo Kluz at the controls, the Potez attacked Dubica, Kostjnica Dvor and Bosanski Novi. More patrols were flown by R-100s as a result, and on 11 June a fighter section equipped with one R-100 and one BH-33 was formed at Dubica airfield specifically to 'destroy the rebel aircraft'. An extensive search was conducted in an effort to locate the Potez on the ground, and a Luftwaffe Focke-Wulf Fw 58, flown by Leutnant Bumb of *SchGr West Bosnien*, finally found it on 7 July near Lusci Palanka. The German aircraft duly destroyed the rebel machine.

Its pilot, Franjo Kluz, later travelled to the Middle East and joined the RAF's No 352 (Yugoslav) Sqn. He was killed in Spitfire VC JK967 on 24 September 1944 when it was downed by flak during an attack on the Yugoslavian port town of Omis.

This Avia BH-33E was photographed at Zaluzani airfield during the summer of 1942. Built in small numbers under licence by the Yugoslavians the early 1930s, the BH-33E was a Czech-designed fighter of the late 1920s. The ZNDH received seven ex-VVKJ BH-33Es, and used them to strafe Partisan and *Chetnik* troops all over NDH (*Authors*)

On 25 June 1943 the ZNDH received reinforcements in the shape of nine Fiat G.50bis (and one G.50B) fighters. These aircraft, together with two IK-2s and six BH-33s, were concentrated at Zaluzani airfield, in Banja Luka, in mid-October, where they stayed for almost a year, flying many strafing missions.

NOP activists were still at work during this period, however, and on 7 October, the CO of 1. *Zrakoplovna Skupina* (Air Group), 12-kill ace boj Mato Culinovic, who had recently returned from service with 15(*Kroat*)./ JG 52, died along with his two crew after partisan-sympathising mechanics connected a bomb detonator to the bomb-bay doors of their Do 17K (Wk-Nr 0101) before an anti-Partisan sortie west of Zagreb. The bomber exploded over the target and its remains fell near the village of Sosica.

By the end of the year the ZNDH had a total of 191 aircraft (including four IK-2, six BH-33s and ten G.50s), but it had lost 49 machines either in combat or due to accidents. And its operations were to be seriously hampered in 1944 by a shortage of fuel, which resulted in orders to curtail flying.

The opposition forces were also suffering setbacks, with a conflict arising between the communist-dominated *Narodnooslobodilacka Vojska Jugoslavije* (NOVJ – People's Liberation Army of Yugoslavia), which included a growing number of Croats, and the pro-monarchy, Serb-dominated *Chetniks*. Taking orders from Moscow, the communists saw their struggle as one not only against the Axis-powers and their satellites, but also as a revolution to change the social foundation of the state post war.

Often, groups of insurgents were at each others' throats, rather than attacking their common enemy. There was even collaboration with the Axis by both sides. In general, though, the policy was to avoid combat whenever possible so as to husband forces in anticipation of an Allied invasion.

By 1943 the fall of Stalingrad had resulting in a massive inflow of new members for the insurgent groups. On Borongaj airfield, three independent cells were formed, and one, led by sat Ivan Cvencek, remained active until war's end. All this subversive activity destabilised the leadership, and General Vladimir Kren was dismissed as head of the ZNDH in mid-September and replaced by ppuk Adalbert Rogulja. The latter initiated a major reorganisation, but the ZDNH's fortunes were little improved.

Following Italy's capitulation in September 1943, around 60 worn-out *Regia Aeronautica* aircraft were found at Mostar and Zadar airfields, and 33 machines were incorporated into the ZNDH. The fighters within this number included six Fiat CR.42s and three more G.50s, and these were loaned to Kro JGr 1 at the beginning of 1944. Then in mid-October 1943, the ZNDH received the first of 38 Morane Saulnier MS 406c-1s that were supplied by the Germans from captured French stock. By the end of the year the Croat-manned air arm had 98 aircraft on strength, including 20 MS 406s, ten G.50s, five BH-33s and two IK-2s.

Although the ZNDH was now able to mount a credible threat against the insurgents, by then a new menace was arriving from the other side of the Adriatic. On 30 June 1943 the first Allied reconnaissance flights were reported, followed by the first USAAF bombers, when 61 B-24s of IX Bomber Command overflew Croatia during a deep-penetration raid on the Austrian city of Wiener Neustadt on 13 August. The 3rd Flak Group, defending Brod na Savi, managed to shoot down a single bomber en route to its target.

GERMAN AMBIVALENCE

Throughout its period of occupation, the German attitude towards their Croat allies was somewhat ambivalent. Indeed, it would be fair to say that the NDH was the most derided of all German satellite countries. For example, as early as May 1941, the Croats had asked for, among other things, 22 Bf 109s. Instead, they got the worst remains of the VVKJ. Yet, at the same time the RLM gave six Do 17Ks to Bulgaria, six Hurricanes and six Blenheims to Rumania and 20 half-completed Blenheims, together with tools and a huge variety of spare parts, to the Finns.

The formation of HZL units by the new NDH regime soon after occupation by the Germans was intended to ensure that the ZNDH received a cadre of qualified airmen, along with modern aircraft. That never happened. In fact, the ZNDH had no control over some of its own units, let alone those of the HZL that were stationed in the NDH. Even tiny Slovakia was held in greater esteem by the Nazis, for that country received its first *Emil*s in 1942, with *Gustav*s following in the spring 1944.

And although the personnel of 13(*Slowakische*)./JG 52 flew Luftwaffe aircraft, they remained part of the Slovak Air Force, wearing Slovak uniforms and staying under Slovak jurisdiction. This was far from the case for the members of 15(*Kroat*)./JG 52.

During the war the Germans made many promises to their Croat allies but kept few of them. The Croat airmen felt this inequality keenly, and their dissatisfaction was to boil over during the summer of 1944. In the meantime, when US aircraft appeared, the best the ZNDH could put up to defend its homeland were Fiat and Morane fighters – aircraft that had been obsolete in 1940!

By the end of 1943 the USAAF's Fifteenth Air Force was regularly overflying the NDH during many of its attacks on Germany and Austria. In a direct response to these flights, on 30 October 11.*Lovacka Skupina* (LS) – consisting of 21. and 22. *Lovacko Jato* (LJ) – was formed at Borongaj airfield. Led by veteran World War 1 fighter pilot boj Ernest Turko, it was equipped with MS 406s and G.50s. Its 23.LJ was duly formed on 26 January 1944, and became operational at Zaluzani airfield at the end of March.

Initially, the RLM decided to equip one operational HZL *Staffel*, which would form part of the *Reichsverteidigung*, together with other *Jagdwaffe* units in the Balkans and Italy, and one training *Staffel*, that was intended to later become an operational unit. On 23 December 1943 the HZL fighter component was reorganised as *Stab*, 1., 2. and 3. *Kroatien Jagdgruppe* 1. The *Gruppenkommandeur* was Major

Pilots of 2./*Kro* JGr 1 in Zagreb in December 1943. They are, from left to right, Ivan Kulic, Asim Korhut, Jakob Petrovic, Bogomir Kunovic, Leopold Hrastovcan, Dragutin Kucinic and Josip Cekovic. They had been sent from JG 104 to 2./Erg JG 1 in Saint-Jean-d'Angely, France, on 1 November 1943, and by 20 December had returned to Zagreb (*Authors*)

Mechanics of 2/*Kro* JGr 1 pose with C.202 'White 4' at Kurilovec airfield in the spring of 1944. The first batch of 16 C.202s delivered to *Kro* JGr 1 were from some 60 XII series aircraft built by Breda after the German occupation. Croat pilots did not have a high opinion of the C.202 due to its light armament of just two 12.7 mm and two 7.7 mm machine guns, which made it ineffective against heavily armed US bombers. The pilots' ability to defend Croatian airspace was also detrimentally affected by the NDH's underdeveloped air-raid warning system, which saw fighters often taking off to intercept attacking bombers when they were already overhead. The CO of 2/JGr *Kro*, Major Helebrant, branded the C.202s as 'old, weary and unusable', and described the morale of his men as 'low, and his unit's results as nil' (*J Novak*)

Ivan Cenic, his *Staffelkapitäne* being Oberleutnant Dukovac (then still on the strength of III./JG 52 in the east), Hauptmann Helebrant and Oberleutnant Bencetic.

3./*Kro* JGr 1 was originally conceived as an operational training unit to supply 2. *Staffel* with combat-ready pilots. Apart from a few veterans from Russia, most of its pilots were fresh from JG 104, and at the end of the year *Kro* JGr 1 had just two non-operational CR.42s in Croatia.

Then, at the end of January 1944, eight brand-new Macchi C.202 fighters arrived at Lucko airfield, with another four flying in two weeks later, although one was lost during a test-flight. In the meantime, operational training on CR.42s and G.50s started as a prelude to C.202 training in March. That month the first contact with American aircraft came west of Zagreb, although combat was avoided – the Macchi pilots were instructed to attack only damaged aircraft and stragglers from the main formation. On 1 April the unit was re-designated I./*Jagdgruppe Kroatien*, just in time for the first combats. The ZNDH also received another 19 MS 406s at this point.

On 2 April the Fifteenth Air Force mounted a large-scale raid on the Austrian industrial city of Steyr. The bombers' route was directly over the NDH, and two 2./JGr *Kro* pilots took off to intercept the B-24s on their return journey. One pilot (almost certainly Eastern Front veteran Feldwebel Bozidar Bartulovic) claimed a bomber, but as its demise was not seen, his victory was not confirmed.

Around this time 2./JGr *Kro* despatched a *Schwarm* to Zaluzani airfield, near Banja Luka, this move, it was assumed, being undertaken in order to give pilots more opportunity for the interception of American bombers. However, on the 6th Spitfire Mk IXs of the South African Air Force's No 7 Wing (specifically Nos 1, 2 and 4 Sqns) made a devastating attack on the airfield. They approached Zaluzani undetected, and thus took the defences completely by surprise.

During the attack, Daut Secerbegovic, then a mechanic with 23.LJ, witnessed the death of Cvitan Galic, Croatia's second-ranking ace with 38 kills. He recalls:

'Aircraft were in the open all across the field, and the hangars were full. Nobody bothered to disperse them because no attack was expected. Galic had just returned from a test flight. He taxied up to the hangar and shut down his engine. An airman helped him release his straps and get out.

'He was standing by his machine when, out of the blue, bullets whistled around us and bombs started going off. We dashed to nearby trenches and dived in just in time. I looked back and saw Galic standing in complete shock. We shouted to him to run to our trench, but he thought it was too far and jumped under his aeroplane instead. Seconds later a bomb exploded near his Morane, which caught fire and collapsed on top of him. Galic was by then beyond help, although I don't think that he could have survived the initial explosion of the bomb in any case.'

The only SAAF unit to use bombs during this attack was No 2 Sqn, and it was one of its pilots who almost certainly accounted for the 38-victory ace.

Elsewhere on the airfield there was complete chaos. No fewer than 21 ZNDH aircraft were written off and ten damaged, whilst 16 Luftwaffe machines (including one C.202, plus another damaged) were also destroyed. 23.LJ practically ceased to exist, as only one of its dozen MS 406s remained intact, with another repairable. Two Macchis returned to Lucko the following day.

In early April pilots of 21.LJ paid dearly for their lack of combat experience, although they survived to tell the tale. A mixed patrol of two G.50bis (por Tomislav Kauzlaric and npr Ivan Gregov) and four MS 406c (npr Marko Veselinovic, por Djuro Gredicak, por Tihomir Simcic and por Serif Mehanovic) fighters was flying at 6,500 ft (2,000 m) near Zagreb, hoping to catch damaged American bombers, when they were bounced by two US fighters.

Only Kauzlaric and Simcic managed to return to Borongaj, Veselinovic and Gredicak both belly-landing after their Moranes' engines overheated during their escape. Mehanovic and Gregov bailed out. Gregov was so shaken that he was given a month's leave and relieved from flying for three months. In fact it had all happened so quickly that some of the survivors reported their attackers as P-38 Lightnings, while others said they had been P-47 Thunderbolts! In actual fact, pilots from both the 325th FG (P-47s) and 82nd FG (P-38s) claimed victories in the area.

On 12 April it was the turn of Borongaj airfield to be attacked, and 21 ZNDH aircraft (including three MS 406s and two G.50s) were destroyed, with a further nine being seriously damaged and 17 slightly damaged. A few days later six CR.42s on a ferry flight from Serbia to join 3./JGr *Kro* were attacked on landing and four damaged, one of which was not repairable. To avoid further losses, all flyable aircraft were ordered to auxiliary airfields early each morning, and they did not return until the evening. This tactic did not spare them, however, for many were written off after damage caused by operations from these rough and primitive airstrips.

The next recorded combat with American aircraft occurred on 23 April. Among that day's targets for the Fifteenth Air Force were the Austrian cities of Wiener Neustadt, Bad Vöslau and Schwechat. Five C.202s, led by Major Ivan Cenic, scrambled from Lucko to intercept the bombers on their return flight, but instead they encountered P-51 Mustangs of the 308th FS/31st FG near Bjelovar. At least two Macchis were shot down by 1Lt Frederick Trafton, although he claimed three kills (see *Osprey Aircraft of the Aces 7 – Mustang Aces of the Ninth and Fifteenth Air Forces and the RAF* for further details). Both pilots – one of them being Cenic himself – bailed out unharmed.

To compensate for these losses, Unteroffizier Leopold Hrastovcan claimed the unit's first confirmed victory when he shot down a B-24 near the village of Zapresic, in Zagorje.

Days later Unteroffizier Jakob Petrovic encountered an RAF Mosquito. He reported:

'Whilst flying with Stjeoan Klaric, we spotted a recce Mosquito flying at 26,000 ft (8,000 m) west of Jastrebarsko. We gained more height and were in a sound position above him when we attacked. I fired a two-second burst and hit him. He started to trail thick smoke and turned towards the sea. At that moment another Mosquito attacked us from above and we had to break off our attack. He didn't bother us much, however, diving off towards Italy. I just managed to see the first one trailing smoke and gently losing height in the distance, but could not follow it as my fuel was getting dangerously low.'

A few weeks later Petrovic again clashed with allied aircraft:

'In early May I was flying with Ivan Kulic on a free hunt. We'd been ordered to patrol over Ljubljana–Triglav–Trieste–Pula–Rijeka–Zagreb at 16,000 ft (5,000 m). After passing Triglav, we saw two Lightnings just beneath us, flying over the coast towards Ljubljana. We made a left turn which positioned us up-sun. I took aim and fired at the starboard aircraft, and I could see my bullets striking its fuselage, and at that moment its stabiliser tore off. The Lightning stalled and fell near Gradiska village, close to the Venice railway line. The pilot did not get out. In the meantime, Kulic had damaged the other one, but it escaped to the south.'

By early May, 3./JGr *Kro* had received four G.50s, two ex-ZNDH MS 406s, a pair of two-seat G.50Bs and at least one Reggiane Re.2002. At around this time six pilots from I./JGr *Kro* were also sent to Nis airfield to collect four C.202s and two C.200s, but one of the C.202s crash-landed near Zemun airfield during the ferry flight. The Remaining three were incorporated into 2./JGr *Kro* and the C.200s went to 3./JGr *Kro*.

ANTI-PARTISAN OPERATION

On 25 May the Luftwaffe launched its biggest operation in Yugoslavia since April 1941 – a combined air and land assault on Drvar, aimed at destroying the partisans' headquarters. A total of 295 aircraft and 45 gliders was assembled for Operation *Rosselsprung*, and the Luftwaffe mounted 440 sorties that day, with another 201 on the 26th.

The Croats were not told about the operation until after it had commenced, as the Germans feared that its details would be passed onto the partisans. No ZNDH units were involved as a result.

Despite this operation, the Germans could not prevent Allied fighters from roaming at will through Croatian skies, targeting NDH airfields. By the 31st, the Allies had destroyed or damaged no less than 93 aircraft in the air and on the ground, about a quarter of which belonged to the

G.50bis '3504' of 2.LJ was photographed at Borongaj in the summer of 1944. The aircraft (which had previously belonged to 21.LJ, with whom it saw extensive service against NOVJ units) served in the ZNDH for over two years, before being severely damaged in a landing accident at Borongaj on 11 August 1944. It was not repaired (*Authors*)

ZNDH, including six MS 406s and one G.50 destroyed at Borongaj on the 30th. The six remaining 2./JGr *Kro* C.202s had been dispersed to Borovo airfield on 29 May. By then Luftwaffe operations as part of *Rosselsprung* had been brought to a halt when it became apparent that their objective was unattainable.

When bad weather over Germany prevented the Fifteenth Air Force from attacking its intended objective of Blechhammer on 30 June, the USAAF 'heavies' turned their attention instead to various targets in Hungary and Yugoslavia. Three recently arrived C.205s, flown by Eastern Front veterans Major Helebrant, Oberleutnant Bencetic and Feldwebel Bartulovic, accompanied by three inexperienced pilots in C.202s, took off to intercept the intruders and received a severe beating.

After encountering the US bombers, and their escorting fighters, over Bjelovar, only Bencetic succeeded in returning to Pleso. The remaining five aircraft were lost, two pilots bailing out and three crash-landing. All, though, survived. Some of the Macchis were lost to the bombers' gunners and others fell to 5th FS/52nd FG Mustangs, although pilots from this group actually claimed two 'Bf 109s' and two 'Fw 190s' 40 miles (60 km) from Bjelovar.

Few documents concerning the operations of 2./JGr *Kro* survive, which is why little is known about its actions, except that its pilots scored four confirmed kills and seven (some sources say 12) unconfirmed victories. Amongst the types claimed shot down were two B-24s and a single B-17, Mosquito, P-38, P-51 and Spitfire. Its successful pilots included Feldwebel Bozidar Bartulovic (unconfirmed B-24 kill) and Unteroffiziere Josip Cekovic (unconfirmed B-24 kill), Leopold Hrastovcan (a B-24 confirmed and an unconfirmed enemy aircraft), Asim Korhut (a B-24 confirmed and an unconfirmed enemy aircraft), Ivan Kulic (a P-38 confirmed and two unconfirmed enemy aircraft) and Jakob Petrovic (a P-38 confirmed and an unconfirmed Mosquito).

On 3 June ,1944 Vladimir Kren returned to his previous position as head of the ZNDH, and three days later he instigated further reorganisation. As a result 11.LS was disbanded, and 2.LJ was formed as a part of 1.ZS in Zagreb, where it was issued with 11.LS's six surviving G.50bis. The

This particular C.202 was one of a batch delivered from *Luftpark Nis*, these machines differing from other Macchis used by the Croats through the application of an RLM 04 fuselage band and identically coloured lower engine cowling. Here, cadets from the ZNDH flying school at Borovo airfield take the opportunity to pose on a 2./JGr *Kro* C.202 in June 1944. They are, from left to right, Zoltan Perisic, Zvonimir Stimac, Stanko Forkapic and Nenad Kovacevic. All except Perisic went to the NOVJ at the beginning of September 1944, and later joined 11.LD (*Authors*)

A ZNDH cadet poses in front of a camouflaged ex-2./JGr *Kro* C.202. Following the HZL's disbandment, most airworthy Macchis were flown by German pilots from Borovo airfield to Borongaj during September 1944 (*M Jeras*)

remaining fighter units were 5.LJ (part of 2.ZS at Rajlovac, with four BH-33Es) and 14.LJ (part of 5.ZS in Banja Luka, but without aircraft). The surviving 28 MS 406s were collected at Borongaj for general repair.

MUTINY

Shortly before 27 June HZL anniversary celebration, the simmering resentment of Croat legionnaires erupted into open mutiny. This was touched off by news that instead of the promised return to the ZNDH, the RLM now planned to equip five HZL *Staffeln* with fighters and bombers and post two to Rumania, two to Italy and one to France! An early result of this was the defection of five men aboard a Do 17.

Then, in a speech to his men, Oberst Dzal bluntly called on those who did not want to stay in the Legion to choose between returning to the ZNDH, going to Germany for further training, or 'going into the woods' as partisans. His words were greeted by whistles and shouts of disapproval. An official report stated that '80 per cent of the men demanded to return to the ZNDH, but for now their wish has been refused'. The result of this general unrest was not long in coming. On 21 July General Kren officially disbanded the HZL, and it was replaced by a new force called the HZS, which was comprised of those who had opted to stay in the Luftwaffe.

By the summer of 1944, the situation facing the Croatian state, both on the ground and in the air, was looking grim. The Allies had gained mastery of the skies, while NOVJ forces controlled most rural areas. More importantly, the influence of the partisans had grown to the extent that whole units of the Croatian Army were deserting. For example, in August 1,000 men of the Air Force School Regiment at Petrovaradin changed sides. Aircraft were also now being flown to Allied-held airfields in increasing numbers, and by the end of 1944, 23 had been lost in this way.

The ZNDH suffered another serious setback at Banja Luka in September when NOVJ's 5th Corps seized Zaluzani airfield, along with 21 aircraft. It was recaptured a week later, along with 17 damaged aircraft which the partisans had failed to destroy. The airworthy machines were hastily evacuated to Sanski Most, from where they continued operations until the unit's disbandment on 22 April 1945.

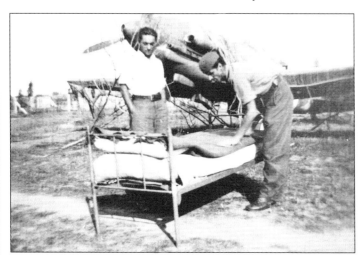

After their barracks was destroyed in a sabotage attack on 22 August 1944, pilots at Borovo had to sleep in the open, although putting a bed in front of an aircraft in those days could hardly have been considered wise (*M Jeras*)

In mid-September the ZNDH received 12 Fieseler Fi 167A-0 biplane attack aircraft, which were incorporated into 1.*Zrakoplovna Skupina* at Borongaj. Built to serve as a torpedo-bomber aboard the still-born German aircraft carrier the *Graf Zeppelin*, the Fieseler's short-field and load-carrying abilities made it ideal for transporting ammunition and other supplies to besieged garrisons.

During one such mission, on 10 October, Fi 167 Wk-Nr 4808, flown by eight-kill ace nar Bozidar Bartulovic, was intercepted by RAF

Morane-Saulnier MS 406c-1 '2323' of *Eskadrila 5. Korpusa* (5th Corps Squadron) is serviced in the open at Sanski Most. It was one of the aircraft captured at Zaluzani on 20 September 1944 and, with the help of ex-ZNDH airmen who had joined the NOVJ, a provisional unit was formed. The French fighter flew 38 sorties against the besieged Kastel fortress, attacking enemy troops on the road between Bosanska Gradiska and Banja Luka from 20 to 27 September. During the course of these sorties, vod Sulejman 'Suljo' Selimbegovic twice encountered Luftwaffe aircraft. On 23 September, flying MS 406c '2332', he intercepted a JuW 34 and an Hs 126B that were dropping supplies at Kastel. Four days later, while evacuating the aircraft to Sanski Most, he came upon two NSGr 7 CR.42s over the village of Bronzani Majdan. Following a brisk exchange of fire, Selimbegovic had to break off combat because of an overheating engine, forcing him to hurriedly landed at Prijedor airfield. It was often stated in post-war literature that he had shot down one or two aircraft during these flights, but there are no records available to substantiate such claims (*Authors*)

Mustang Mk IIIs of No 213 Sqn near Sisak. The pilot reported that five fighters made two passes on him, setting the aircraft alight and wounding him in the head. His gunner, sat Mate Jurkovic, claimed one of the attackers before both men had to bail out. British records state that a 'single-engined biplane, possibly an Fi 167' was shot down over Martinska Ves by Sqn Ldr Clifford Vos (in Mustang III HB902) and Sgts W E Mould (KH554) and D E Firman (FB337). Sgt Mould's aircraft was hit and wrecked in a subsequent crash-landing.

During the same period, another 'unidentified single-engined biplane' was claimed near Glina by Vos, Firman and Sgt W H Butterworth (HB854). This was actually a ZNDH Bu 131 Jungmann on its way from Zagreb to Bihac.

On 24 November the ZNDH finally received its first Bf 109G-14AS. Its arrival followed in the wake of a visit to Berlin in October by General Kren, during which the delivery of 150 aircraft – including ten Bf 109G-6s, ten G-10s and ten G-14s – had been agreed. The new aircraft were allocated to 1. *Zrakoplovna Skupina*'s (commanded by boj Zlatko Stipcic) 2.LJ (CO sat Ljudevit Bencetic) and 14.LJ (CO sat Vid Sajic). At the time these were the sole operational ZNDH fighter units.

Under a further reorganisation on 21 December, 1. *Zrakoplovna Lovacka Skupina* was formed under the command of boj Josip Helebrant. It was to be manned by HZIS pilots training to fight as infantry in Poland, who, according to German promises, would return to Croatia by the end of the year. However, these men did not return until early 1945, and the unit never became operational – when the HZIS pilots did finally make it back to Croatia, they were assigned to 2.LJ.

At the Germans' request, 2.LJ moved to Borongaj on 16 December, but six aircraft were allowed to return to Lucko on the 25th. By year-end four *Gustav*s had already been written-off in accidents and acts of sabotage, with two pilots being injured. On 28 December partisans, with inside help supplied by boj Ivan Cvencek, destroyed four Do 17s together with Croat leader Ante Pavelic's personal Ju 52, and damaged several Bf 109s at an auxiliary airfield near Borongaj. Boj Stipcic was held responsible and dismissed, and his place as CO of 1.ZS was in turn taken by Cvencek himself!

TERRIBLE YEAR

1944 had been a catastrophic year for the ZNDH. Aircraft losses amounted to 234, and it entered 1945 with 196 machines, including 17 Bf 109Gs (12 operational), 12 MS 406s (two operational), seven G.50s (two operational) and two CR.42s, neither of which was operational.

The order for 30 Messerschmitts was expanded by ten Bf 109K-4s and four G-12 two-seaters, and it was planned to exchange all the G-models

for Bf 109Ks the following spring. Two of the new aircraft were lost after colliding during a ferry flight in bad weather, and two K-4s and a G-12 were damaged on arrival in deep snow. Two pilots were injured in these accidents, one seriously.

Initially, these aircraft were used sparingly on reconnaissance, bomber escort and free hunt sorties. The tempo of operations quickened from 10 March, by which time 2.LJ had returned to Lucko, and the ZNDH was operating 23 Bf 109s, six G.50s, three MS 406s and two Bf 110s.

On 24 March vod Asim Korhut and vod Ivan Mihaljevic were attacked by five RAF Spitfires (probably from No 73 Sqn) between Sisak and Petrinja. Korhut managed to escape, but Mihaljevic – who had returned to Croatia just ten days earlier – was hit and crash-landed his Bf 109G-14 ('Black 8' Wk-Nr 2108) near the village of Hrastovice. He died from his wounds before help could arrive.

That same day, eight RAF Mustangs of Nos 213 and 249 Sqns attacked Lucko airfield using napalm bombs. One No 213 Sqn aircraft was brought down by flak, and although the returning pilots claimed two Fw 190s and one Ju 88 destroyed, plus one unidentified aircraft damaged, on the ground, their actual score was far higher. The ZNDH had lost three Bf 109s and one MS 406 destroyed and the Luftwaffe an Fw 190. In addition, three ZNDH Bf 109s, three G.50s and a single Bf 108, Bf 110 and MS 406 had been damaged, as had two Fw 190s, one Ju 88 and several Bf 109s and Hs 126s of the Luftwaffe.

There were to be further losses the next day when vod Korhut, flying a Bf 109G-10, and his wingman vod Ivan Misulin, in a G.50, fled with their aircraft to an RAF-held airfield.

On 30 March four *Gustav*s escorted a similar number of Do 17s attacking 4.JA partisan army positions near Gospic. Warned by Boj

The ZNDH received 12 Fieseler Fi 167A-0 multi-purpose attack aircraft in mid-September 1944, and on the 25th of that same month boj Adum Romeo and boj Matija Petrovic used Fi 167A '4807' to defect to Topusko airfield. Petrovic had previously helped leading Croat ace Mato Dukovac arrange details for his safe defection to the Soviet side just five days earlier. Petrovic's Fi 167A-0 aircraft was incorporated into *Eskadrila za vezu Vrhovnog Staba* NOVJ (NOVJ HQ Liaison Squadron), based at the RAF airfield at Vis. It was mistakenly shot down by SAAF Mustangs on 17 October 1944 near Vrdovo village, its pilot, Miljenko Lipovscak, and two crewmen surviving the attack, although their passenger, Gen Vladimir Djetkovic, CO of 8th Corps, NOVJ, did not (*HPM*)

Cvencek, the RAF duly scrambled Spitfires from No 73 Sqn, and two Do 17s (Wk-Nrs 0401 and 0411) were shot down, although the Croat fighters escaped into the clouds, with only the Bf 109G-14 of vod Antun Plese being slightly damaged. This brought total ZNDH losses for the first three months of 1945 to 59 aircraft, including 15 Bf 109s, ten MS 406s, two CR.42s and two G.50s. At the same time it had received 39 new aircraft.

There were further clashes with RAF Spitfires on 2 April, when four *Gustav*s were sent to attack JA forces near the village of Medak. The first pair, comprising Bencetic and Jelak, made one strafing pass and left, but the second was intercepted by No 73 Sqn Spitfire Mk IXs. Canadian Plt Off Norman John Pearce shot down the leading aircraft and it crash-landed in no-man's land near Primislje. The pilot evaded capture, soldiers finding only the aircraft and a Luftwaffe flying-jacket with major's rank badges. The missing pilot was probably 12-kill ace boj Zlatko Stipcic, who was known for his penchant for Luftwaffe gear. One other aircraft was claimed as damaged, which may have been that of an unknown pilot who belly-landed at Lucko.

On 16 April, four *Gustav*s took off from Lucko on a reconnaissance mission. Over Sinj, nar Vladimir Sandtner in Bf 109G-10 'Black 4' (Wk-Nr 2104) and nar Josip Cekovic in Bf 109G-14 'Black 10' (Wk-Nr 2110) fell behind and headed for Italian airfields – Sandtner landed at Falconara and Cekovic at Jesi. Four days later two out of four *Gustav*s on a mission to attack JA units landed at Mostar. There, nar Vinko Tatarevic, (Bf 109G-10 'Black 3' Wk-Nr 2103) and 11-kill ace boj Josip Helebrant (Bf 109G-14 'Black 5 ' Wk-Nr 2105) were immediately incorporated into a unit called the Mostar Squadron, with Helebrant was made its deputy CO.

On 23 April 15-kill ace sat Ljudevit Bencetic (Bf 109G-10 'Black 22' Wk-Nr 2122) and por Mihajlo Jelak (Bf 109G-14 'Black 27' Wk-Nr 2127) claimed two RAF Mustangs of No 213 Sqn shot down near Zagreb, but Jelak's aircraft was in turn hit and he crash-landed near Velika Gorica. These were the final aerial kills credited to Croatian pilots in World War 2.

That same day the last Bf 109 (a K-4) was delivered to the ZNDH, while vod Milan Grm, recently arrived from JG 108, defected. He

Bf 109G-10 'Black 3' of *Mostarska Eskadrila* (Mostar Squadron) is seen in the dispersal area at Mostar airfield with two RAF Dakotas in the spring of 1945. On 20 April 1945 boj Helebrant and nar Tatarevic had defected to JA-held Mostar, where both pilots were incorporated into *Mostarska Eskadrila*. They flew their first combat sorties on 7 May, escorting bombers and strafing *Chetnik* troops. This mission was repeated the next day, and in the afternoon the unit transferred to Rajlovac airfield. On the 9th both pilots again strafed retreating *Chetniks*, but the weather deteriorated during their return flight and Helebrant and Tatarevic got lost. They managed to force-land north of the Sava river, heavily damaging their *Gustavs* in the process (*S Ostric*)

Marked with the distinctive 'Zvonimir' cross, Bf 109G-14AS 'Black 17' of 2.LJ is kept locked away in a hangar at Lucko airfield in the spring of 1945. JA units found nine ZNDH, Luftwaffe and *Magyar Kiralyi Honved Legiero* (Hungarian) *Gustavs* at Lucko following the surrender of Axis forces in the area (*Authors*)

belly-landed his *Gustav* at Jelas, near Brod na Savi, and escaped to join his family.

In the days that followed there was little aerial combat, but pilots were still dying. The final ZNDH fighter pilot loss came on 6 May when por Mihajlo Jelak and vod Leopold Hrastovcan, in two ancient R-100 training fighters, bombed a railway bridge over the Kupa river in an effort to stop the JA advance on Karlovac. Hrastovcan's aircraft was hit by ground fire and he force-landed near his target. He was captured and shot on the spot.

That evening, sat Ljudevit Bencetic gathered his men together at Lucko and told them that they were released from their oath of loyalty, and that each was free to go. The next morning Bencetic took off for Austria with the sole flyable Bf 109, although unbeknown to him the fighter had been sabotaged during the night and he was forced to crash-land at Cerklje airfield.

Altogether, 2.LJ had flown some 150 combat and 450 training sorties in its Bf 109s during the war's closing stages.

By early April 1945 the JA had liberated large areas of Yugoslavia, and was advancing towards Zagreb and Ljubljana. The roads were full of pro-Nazi personnel retreating westwards, and there was complete chaos. Many airmen, meanwhile, headed for JA-held airfields or Allied bases in Italy and Austria, whilst others joined the general retreat, hoping to surrender to British or US troops. Zagreb was liberated on 6 May 1945, the day the war in Europe ended, but some *Ustasa* forces managed to hold out in Bosnia until the 25th.

Most of the captured ZNDH personnel, including some taken by the British, were sent on a 300-mile (500-km) forced march to prison camps in Vojvodina. Not all survived. A general amnesty was proclaimed on 15 May, but men were rounded up and imprisoned, sometimes for many

years. High-ranking ZNDH officers, especially known *Ustasa* supporters, were court-martialled and sentenced to death.

Many Croat pilots, however, contributed to the Allied victory in World War 2. Some fighter pilots joined the RAF or the newly formed JRV, and although none of them became aces, this is not to belittle their deeds, or their sacrifices.

Against the wishes of the pro-monarchist Yugoslav government in exile, and of many former VVKJ members, the British government sanctioned the formation of two pro-NOVJ Yugoslav squadrons within the RAF in 1944. They comprised former VVKJ and PV airmen who had escaped to Egypt in 1941, former *Regia Aeronautica* prisoners of war of Slavic origin, NOVJ fighters in Yugoslavia and ZNDH and HZL defectors.

On 22 April 1944, No 352 (Yugoslav) Sqn was formed at Benina, in Libya, and after training, its 16 Spitfire VB/VC fighters arrived at Canne, in southern Italy, on 12 August. The unit was incorporated into No 281 Wing, Balkan Air Force, and flew its first combat sortie on 18 August. In 1945 the unit moved firstly to Vis airfield and then to Prkos, near Zadar. Most of the missions that were flown saw the Spitfire pilots bombing and strafing in support of troops on the ground, and enemy aircraft were encountered only twice.

On 20 March, after bombing *Wehrmacht* columns, Sqn Ldr Hinko Sojic (Spitfire MH592), Plt Offs Sime Fabijanovic (JG871) and Mirko Kovacic (LZ830) and Flt Sgt Mehmedalija Losic (BR130) encountered an Hs 126B of 1./NAGr *Kroatien* and shot it down. All bar Sojic had previously been ZNDH members. Six days later, while escorting USAAF C-47s near Metlika, two pilots claimed a probable kill during a brisk encounter with three Fw 190F-8s of SG 2. Finally, on 20 April, two Spitfires attacked Luco airfield, where they destroyed a ZNDH MS 406 and damaged several other aircraft on the ground.

By 9 May No 352 Sqn had flown 367 missions, but it had also suffered grievous losses. Of the 27 pilots assigned to the unit, three died in training and seven in action. Only four Croats flew with the squadron, namely Sqn Ldr Hinko Sojic (73 sorties), Plt Offs Sime Fabijanovic (66 sorties) and Franjo Kluz (killed on 24 September 1944 during his 12th

Spitfire VC MA340 of No 352 (Yugoslav) Sqn was photographed at Prkos airfield on 26 March 1945. Built by Vickers-Armstrongs at Castle Bromwich in April 1943, this aircraft had seen considerable service in the Mediterranean with other RAF fighter units (namely Nos 601, 73 and 87 Sqns, as well as No 3 Sqn SAAF) prior to its transfer to No 352 Sqn in the spring of 1944. The fighter was eventually withdrawn from service in 1946 (*S Ostric*)

Yak-9T 'White 81' of 111.LP was photographed at Kupusina airfield, near Sombor, during operations on the Srem Front in April 1945. The six stars beneath the cockpit indicate that it was flown by an unnamed VVS SSSR ace from 236.IAD prior to it being transferred to 11.LD. Yugoslav markings were applied to these Yaks post-war (*M Micevski*)

Two ex-ZNDH pilots shake hands in front of Yak-3 'Yellow 12' of 113.LP at Ljubljana in September 1945. To the left is Maj Miljenko Lipovscak, CO of 113.LP, who had defected to the Partisans in early 1943. To the right is por Andrija Arapovic, CO of I *Eskadrila* 113.LP, who had landed his G.50bis '3505' at RAF Vis on 2 September 1944. The aircraft behind them had previously been the mount of Soviet ace, and CO of 267.IAP, ppol Sergei Sergeyevich Shchirov, and it still carries his personal markings (*M Micevski*)

sortie) and Sgt Zvonimir Halambek (killed in action on 1 July 1944). Six ex-ZNDH pilots of other nationalities also saw considerable action with No 352 Sqn.

No 351 (Yugoslav) Sqn

Formed at Benina on 1 July 1944, No 351 (Yugoslav) Sqn was equipped with Hurricane Mk IVRP fighter-bombers. By 10 October the unit had completed its move to Canne, where it remained until war's end, although it used Vis and Prkos as forward airstrips.

The unit was primarily involved in rocket and strafing missions, and it flew some 971 sorties – four pilots died and one was captured during these operations. Of the squadron's 23 pilots, four were Croats, namely Plt Off Josip Klokocovnik (50 sorties) and Sgts Ljubomir Dvorski (62 sorties), Vladimir Pavicic (56 sorties) and Tugomir Prebeg (45 sorties). Four others were former ZNDH members.

In September 1944 agreement was reached with the Soviet Union under which the JRV would receive enough fighters to equip two air force divisions. Aircraft came from Soviet 17. Air Army, and by year's end 42. *Jurisna* and 11.*Lovacka Divizija* (LD – assault and fighter division) had been formed.

11.LD's Iinitial equipment comprised 103 Yak-1bs, 14 Yak-9s, three Yak-3s and one Yak-7B, with 20 more Yakovlev fighters arriving during January 1945. Three *Lovacki Puk* (fighter regiments) were formed, 111. 112. and 113.

The Yugoslav pilots of 11.LD flew their first combat sortie on 20 January 1945 in support of troops fighting on the Srem Front in Croatia, Bosnia and Slovenia. Most operations involved *Stormovik* escort and strafing missions, and although Luftwaffe aircraft were occasionally encountered, no victories were ever achieved. The JRV's Yaks flew their last sortie of the war – a reconnaissance mission over the Yugoslav–Austrian border – on 15 May from Pleso.

A significant number of Croats were included within the 150 pilots that saw service with 11.LD, and no fewer than 45 of these were ex-members of the ZNDH and HZL. Three were killed, two of these during training (Lovro Martincic and Josip Novacek) and vod Josip Grabar to flak near Doboj on 6 April in his Yak-1b, coded 22 (no 48149).

CROATIAN ACES – THE HALL OF FAME

A total of 21 Croatian fighter pilots scored five or more confirmed aerial kills during World War 2, and are therefore entitled to be called aces. Of the 21, 15 were credited with ten or more victories. The combined confirmed score of all the aces was 284 kills, the great majority of which were achieved while flying the Bf 109 on the Eastern Front with the Luftwaffe against the Soviet Union.

This chapter examines the careers of the 21 aces and, where appropriate, what happened to them post war. For a full kill list of all Croatian fighter pilots see the appendices.

It should be stressed that some uncertainty surrounds the claims of 15(*Kroat*)./JG 52, for many of the unit's victories remained unconfirmed, while others were only confirmed many months later. There were also many different levels of claim qualification – confirmed, unconfirmed, allowed, disallowed, probable, possible, witnessed and unwitnessed.

Another difficulty in assessing the unit's success is the conflict between Luftwaffe and ZNDH records, which led to so much post war confusion that even today some pilots' scores remain uncertain. For example, an official ZNDH document confirming Mato Dukovac's score to be 44 kills was found recently at the *Vojno-istorijski institut* (Military Archive) in Belgrade, but it is not known whether the RLM credited him with the same tally of confirmed kills.

It should also be noted that HZL pilots were no better at aircraft recognition than their counterparts in other air arms. This probably explains the disproportionate number of LaGG-3s to Yaks among the claims, when both types were in Soviet service in equal numbers. Similarly, claims for MiG-3s were made at times, and in particular theatres, when such aircraft were not employed.

Mato Dukovac (44 kills)

Born on 23 September 1918 in Surcin, near Zemun, Dukovac had been a keen glider pilot prior to entering the 67th class of the Royal Yugoslav Military Academy in 1937. He graduated on 1 April 1940 with the rank of potporucnik, and was selected for pilot training at 1. *Pilotska Skola* (PS – pilot school) in October 1940. During the April War he served with 2.*eskadrilla* of the *Armijsko vazduhoplovstvo* (army air force) at Velika Gorica airfield.

Dukovac joined the ZNDH with the rank of porucnik on 29 April 1941, and was posted to A/B 120 in October. The following April he started additional training for fighter school, and transferred to JFS 4 in June. Posted to 15(*Kroat*)./JG 52 in October, Dukovac shot down a

Top-scoring Croatian ace Oberleutnant Mato Dukovac poses in the cockpit of his Bf 109G at Bagerovo in November 1943. He was decorated with the *Deutsch Kreutz* in Gold on 29 March 1944 whilst still a patient in a Viennese hospital, recovering from wounds he had received when shot down on 25 February. Dukovac had claimed his 44th, and last, kill earlier in that same mission
(*Bundesarchiv* via D Bernad)

Leutnant Cvitan Galic poses for a propaganda photograph on the wing of Bf 109G 'Yellow 6' at Taman on 6 May 1943. He claimed ten confirmed and two unconfirmed kills during his second combat tour in the East, at least eight of them while flying 'Yellow 6'
(*W Radinger* via D Bernad)

solitary I-16 prior to the unit's withdrawal to Croatia. During its second tour, he claimed 14 confirmed and six unconfirmed victories. As a nad-porucnik, and the newly promoted CO of 15.*Staffel*, Dukovac was posted back to the Eastern Front for the third time on 21 October 1943.

On 25 February 1944 he claimed his last kill (a Yak-9), but on the fifth mission of the day he was in turn shot down by Airacobras and wounded. At that time he had 37 confirmed and eight unconfirmed victories (seven of which were later confirmed) to his credit. Promoted to satnik 'for outstanding achievement on the Eastern Front' on 13 July 1944, Dukovac remained in command of the unit at various bases throughout eastern Europe until he defected to Soviet-controlled territory on 20 September.

Dukovac returned to Belgrade in December as a kapetan with the JRV, and after converting to Yak fighters, he was posted as an instructor to 1.PS in Zadar in April 1945.

On 8 August he defected again when he flew a Tiger Moth to Italy. After spending time in a refugee camp, Dukovac joined the Syrian Air Force in 1946. During the first Arab-Israeli War in 1948, he was a captain in No 1 Fighter Squadron, based at Estabal in the Lebanese Bekaa Valley, where he flew combat missions in T-6 Texans. He subsequently emigrated to Canada and he started a business career. Mato Dukovac died in Toronto in September 1990.

His final wartime tally of kills included a single I-16, MiG-3, Spitfire, La-5, Yak-9, Pe-2 and A-20, two Yak-1s and two DB-3s, three Airacobras, 12 Il-2/Il-2M3s and 18 LaGG-3 (plus one unconfirmed). Dukovac completed 255 sorties, and was involved in 62 aerial engagements. With 44 confirmed victories to his credit, he was the top-scoring Croat pilot of World War 2.

Cvitan Galic (38 kills)

Born on 5 May 1909 in the village of Gorica, Galic completed pilot training with 7. *Vazduhoplovni Puk* (VP – aviation regiment) at Mostar on 1 November 1930, and became a fighter pilot with 6.LP on 1 August 1935.

When Germany invaded, he was serving with Mostar-based III PS. Galic enlisted in the ZNDH in May, and volunteered for the HZL when it was formed. He claimed 24 confirmed, seven unconfirmed (four later confirmed) and two ground victories to become 15(*Kroat*)./JG 52's top scorer during its first combat tour. By 22 October 1942 Galic had advanced four ranks from narednik to porucnik.

In the spring of 1943 he scored a further ten confirmed and two unconfirmed kills. For these exploits, the Germans awarded Galic the

Deutsch Kreutz in Gold on 23 June. During July, as a nadporucnik, he was sent to JG 104 to instruct young Croat pilots. On 20 October he returned to ZNDH, being posted to 22.ZJ, equipped with MS 406s and G.50s at Borongaj.

In December, after visiting his family in Bjelovar, Galic flew back to Zagreb in a PVT trainer, but being 'not very sober', he fell asleep, only to wake up just in time to make a crash-landing in partisan-held territory. Having disposed of his flying gear, he was able to persuade his captors that he was also a partisan. He escaped after 48 hours and

returned to his unit, but only his previous record saved him from harsh punishment. Galic became CO of 23.ZJ (equipped with 12 MS 406s) on 14 March 1944.

Cvitan Galic was killed on 6 April 1944 during an attack on Zaluzani airfield by South African Air Force Spitfires, and posthumously promoted to satnik two weeks later. In 439 sorties on the Eastern Front, Galic claimed a single DB-3, Pe-2, Spitfire and R-10, two MDR-6 flying boats, five Il-2s, four MiG-1s, four I-153s, five I-16s, five MiG-3s and nine LaGG-3s.

Franjo Dzal (16 kills)

Born on 9 April 1909 in Bihac, Dzal initially attended observer school at Petrovaradin in 1927, prior to being accepted into pilot school at 1.VP in Novi Sad the following year. He became a fighter pilot with 6.LP in Zemun in 1931. Already a member of *Ustasa,* Dzal was deputy CO of 5.LP on the outbreak of war.

His tunic bedecked with decorations, Cvitan Galic displays his various claps and medals in late 1942. Below his Luftwaffe wings on his right breast pocket is the HZL badge, the 'Winged Croat Shield'. The medal attached to his top button is the *Hrvatski zeljezni trolist III reda sa hrastovim grancicama* (the Croat Iron Three-leaf 3rd class with Oak Leaves). Finally, on his left breast pocket is a *Frontflug-Spange fur Jager in Silber, Hrvatski zeljezni trolist IV reda* (Croat Iron Three-leaf 4th class), *Velika srebrna kolajna Poglavnika Ante Pavelica za hrabrost* (Grand Silver Medal of Leader Ante Pavelic for courage), *EK I klasse* and ZNDH and Luftwaffe pilot badges (*HPM*)

Oberstleutnant Dzal climbs from the cockpit of 'Black 1'. He was the second-highest scoring Croatian ace during 15(*Kroat*)./JG 52's first combat tour on the Eastern Front (*HPM*)

This photograph of Franjo Dzal was taken during a ceremony in Zagreb on 23 December 1942 (*S Ostric*)

He joined the ZNDH as a bojnik on 29 April 1941, and the HZL in July. Dzal became the first CO of 15(*Kroat*)./JG 52, and in October 1941 was promoted to podpukovnik. Between then and November 1942 he claimed 16 confirmed and three to five unconfirmed victories during the course of 157 missions, but achieved no further kills during his second tour in 1943, since he rarely flew and drank heavily. Dzal became HZL CO on 22 May, but was replaced and sent back to Croatia on 16 June to perform secondary duties with the ZNDH. However, in November 1943 he was made CO of the HZL for the second time.

Promoted to pukovnik in February 1944, Dzal returned the following month to ZNDH HQ as operations officer. Eventually captured in Slovenia by units of 3rd JA towards the end of the war, he was court-martialled in Belgrade and executed in October 1945.

Ljudevit Bencetic (15 kills)

Born on 26 December 1910 in Zagreb, Bencetic graduated from 7.VP in Mostar in 1930 and became a military pilot in 1932. He was promoted to nizi vojno-tehnicki cinovnik III klase (equivalent to porucnik) in December 1940.

At the outbreak of war Bencetic was on non-flying duty with 12. *Bazna Ceta Vazduhoplovnog Zavoda* (base company of air force arsenal) in Kraljevo. He joined the ZNDH in May 1941, and transferred to the HZL in July with the rank of nadporucnik. During his first combat tour Bencetic scored 14 confirmed victories and one unconfirmed kill. During his second tour he added one confirmed and one unconfirmed kill. By the end of 1943 he had flown a total of 250 missions, and had also served as an instructor with JG 104 at Fürth between July and September of that year.

Later employed on ferry duties with *Flugzeugüberführungs Geschwader* 1 at Wiener Neustadt, before being put in command of 3./*Kroatien Jagdgruppe* 1 (later renamed 3./JGr *Kro*) in December, Bencetic was promoted to satnik the following February. In September 1944, following the disbanding of most HZL units, he moved to 5. *Zrakoplovna Luka* (air base) Zaluaeani to command its MS 406-equipped 14.LJ. Bencetic flew three combat missions against the NOVJ and then engaged in ground battles with advancing partisan forces.

Given command of 13. *Zrakoplovno Jato* (air squadron) at Bjelovar airfield, Bencetic was made CO of Borongaj-based 2.LJ in November 1944. He became the last Croatian pilot to claim an aerial victory in World War 2 when he downed an RAF Mustang on 23 April 1945 east of Zagreb. Bencetic then escaped to Austria, but was returned by the British to face a court-martial in Zagreb. Granted amnesty in July 1945, he moved to

Ljudevit 'Lujo' Bencetic is seen in the German Alps in early 1943 (*S Ostric*)

Germany, where his wife, ex-Luft-waffe *helferin* Hella Stampa, awaited him. Ljudevit Bencetic duly changed his name to Ludwig Stampa and died in the late 1980s in Mainz Kastel.

An official photograph of VVKJ pilot Safet Boskic in 1935. His marks during his 'wings' course were above average, and he subsequently served as an instructor at various flying training schools (*MJV*)

Safet Boskic (13 kills)

Born on 31 January 1909 in Fojnica, Bosnian Muslim 'Slavko' Boskic graduated from pilot school in 1932, became a military pilot in 1935 and a fighter pilot in 1938. Enlisted in the ZNDH as a stozerni narednik in July 1941, he joined the HZL soon afterwards.

Boskic claimed all of his victories (13 confirmed, three unconfirmed and one on the ground) during his first combat tour. Promoted to porucnik in October 1942, the following spring he became technical officer for 15(*Kroat*)./JG 52. After service with JG 104 and Fl.Ü.G. 1, Boskic was made technical officer of *Stab/Kro* JGr 1 in December 1943, and in July of the following year technical officer for the whole of the HZS. He headed 2. *Tehnicka Satnija* (technical company) near Vienna from the autumn of 1944, and was promoted to nadporucnik the following December.

Boskic served in the Legion longer than any other Croatian officer, and went into captivity on its disbandment. Released in July 1945, he spent the rest of his life living in Zagreb, remaining active in the local flying club. 'Slavko' Boskic died in 1980.

Zlatko Stipcic (13 kills)

Born on 27 December 1908 in Krizevci, Stipcic was a very gifted painter, although he chose a career in the military instead and became an observer in 1933 – he graduated from pilot school the following year. During 1940 Stipcic flew with 162.LE/6.LP, and duly led 6.LP's fast fighters transition course, before transferring to III PS at Nis. He flew six missions against attacking Ger-man and Italian aircraft in April 1941, claiming a Ju 88 destroyed and a Cant Z. 1007 damaged.

Stipcic joined the ZNDH as a satnik in April 1941, and then the HZL in July. He opened his score in

Hauptmann Zlatko Stipcic is seen at at Mariupol in late 1941. After damaging a Luftwaffe bomber by mistake in October 1941, having already shot another one down in April 1941, he was banned from flying for six months, although he was quickly able to restore his reputation as a fighter pilot of note once the ban was lifted (*J Novak*)

Senior officers of 3. Combined Aviation Brigade VVKJ at Petrovac in 1940. At the extreme left is maj Leonid Bajdak, a Russian who later held senior rank in the ZNDH and gen Vlassov's pro-Axis ROA (Russian Liberation Army) Air Force. Third from left is Mato Culinovic, CO of 205.BE. He was killed in one of 11 ex-VVKJ Do 17Ks inherited by the ZNDH on 7 October 1942. He was much admired by his subordinates (*P Bosnic*)

This official photo shows Mato Culinovic as a VVKJ pilot in 1931. Well known for his prowess at aerobatics pre-war, he competed a few times in the King's Race, but failed to achieve any results of note (*MJV*)

May 1942, and was credited with 12 confirmed and two unconfirmed kills in less than two months. He returned to Croatia in September and received promotion to nadsatnik. Stipcic served mainly as a staff officer during his second tour of the Eastern Front, which commenced in the spring of 1943. Made CO of the re-established 11.ZLJ (later 12.ZLJ) in May, he spent the summer with JG 104 and Fl.Ü.G. 1.

In December Stipcic moved to HZL HQ and was promoted to bojnik in February 1944. He later served as HZS liaison officer in East Prussia. After Dukovac's defection, Stipcic returned to Croatia and command of 1.ZS. He flew combat missions from Borongaj and Lucko, and also tested a captured Spitfire IX. Dismissed on 30 December and imprisoned for ten days, Stipcic continued to fly combat missions with 2.ZJ after his release. Remaining in Zagreb after the war, and joining the JRF, Stipcic was killed by a sentry in an accidental shooting in 1946.

Mato Culinovic (12 kills)

Born on 8 June 1907 near Zagreb, Culinovic graduated from pilot school in 1928, became a military pilot in 1931 and a fighter pilot in 1937. A pre-war *Ustasa* member, he was made CO of 205.BE and promoted to major in April 1941.

Enlisted in the ZNDH in July with the rank of bojnik, Culinovic went to JFS 4 in Fürth on 19 August. Deputy CO of 15(*Kroat*)./JG 52 when it was posted to the Eastern Front in October, Culinovic shot down two I-16s on one day in February 1942, and by July of that year his score stood at 12 confirmed and six unconfirmed kills. He returned to Croatia in August, and the following month took command of 1.ZS at Borongaj airfield. Culinovic was killed on 7 October 1942 when NOP-sympathising groundcrew sabotaged his Do 17K and it blew up in flight.

Veca Mikovic (12 kills)

An official portrait of nar llk Veca Mikovic, taken when he graduated from 2.PS at Kraljevo in 1939 (*MJV*)

Born on 7 January 1914 in Subotica, Mikovic became an aviation mechanic in 1938, graduated from 2.PS in September 1939 and joined III PS in Nis in November 1940. He entered the ZNDH as a vodnik in May 1941 and the HZL in July, and had advanced in rank to narednik by September. In December Mikovic arrived on the Eastern Front, and he opened his score in March 1942 with two I-16s shot down on the same day. On 7 April he and Cvitan

Veca Mikovic climbs out of Bf 109E-3 'Green 15' on 20 June 1942. He died exactly a month later whilst attacking a lone Petlyakov Pe-2 bomber (*J Novak*)

Galic became the war's first Croatian aces. By the time of his death in combat on 20 July 1942, Mikovic had attained the rank of stozerni narednik, and his score stood at ten confirmed and four unconfirmed victories, two of which were later upgraded.

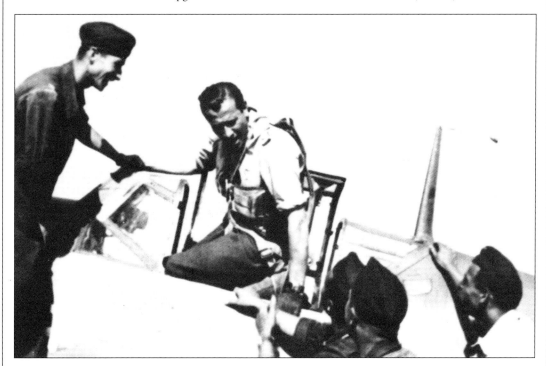

Eduard Martinko (12 kills)

Born on 2 September 1917 near Karlovac, Martinko was part of the Czech minority in Yugoslavia, and he became a naval aviation mechanic with the rank of podnarednik in September 1939. Posted to the PV's 1. *Hidroeskadrila* (seaplane squadron), which was equipped with SIM-XIV seaplanes, he remained on strength with the unit until the collapse of Yugoslavia in April 1941. The following month Martinko joined the ZNDH as a vodnik, and he served as a mechanic in Sarajevo and Petrovaradin until eventually accepted for pilot training at 1.DPJ, in Borongaj.

Promoted to narednik in October, Martinko graduated from A/B 123 and JG 104 as a fighter pilot and joined 15(*Kroat*)./JG 52 for its third combat tour in October 1943. He subsequently claimed ten confirmed and three unconfirmed victories, two of which were later confirmed, in just 24 sorties, but he also suffered five crash landings. Badly hurt in the last of these accidents in early January 1944, Martinko was admitted to hospital in Germany. Promoted to stozerni narednik, he returned to 1/JGr *Kro* (as his unit had become, now based in Croatia) in the spring.

Martinko moved to 2.LJ at Lucko in April 1945, but was restricted to training flights only. He duly graduated from an aviation officers' course just in time to be captured in Slovenia and marched to a prisoner of war camp near the Rumanian border. Martinko died in Zagreb in the 1970s, having never fully recovered from the injuries he suffered in his numerous crash-landings, or from his maltreatment whilst in captivity.

Stjepan Martinasevic (11 kills)

Born on 14 December 1913 in Brod na Savi, Martinasevic trained as an aviation mechanic in 1934 with the rank of narednik. Gaining his pilot's wings the following year, he became a fully fledged military pilot in 1938.

Stjepan Martinasevic (second from left) poses with other pilots in front of a Potez Po 25 A2 Jupiter at Mostar airfield in the late 1930s (*A Ognjevic*)

An official portrait of nar Stjepan Martinasevic, taken in 1935. When war broke out in Yugoslavia he was serving as an instructor with III PS in Mostar (*MJV*)

When Germany invaded he was serving as an instructor with III PS, and he joined the ZNDH in July 1941 and later the HZL, where he received promotion to stozerni narednik. Martinasevic made his first claim (an I-16) in March 1942, and by September his score had risen to 11. He had also by then been promoted to castnicki namjesnik. Martinasevic failed to add to his score during his second combat tour, and after spending three months as an instructor with JG 104, he was promoted to the rank of zastavnik and joined Fl.Ü.G. 1. Whilst serving

81

CROATIAN ACES – THE HALL OF FAME

with the latter unit, Martinasevic ferried aircraft all over south-eastern Europe until he was killed in a flying accident caused by bad weather near Belgrade on 23 December 1943.

Hauptmann Josip Helebrant, CO of 2./*Kro* JGr 1, was photographed at his home in Zagreb in late 1943. He was known as a calm and frank individual, who was very popular with his men (*S Ostric*)

Josip Helebrant (11 kills)

Born in Karlovac on 14 October 1910, Helebrant initially trained as an observer before receiving his pilot's wings in 1936 upon graduation from 1.VP in Novi Sad.

Promoted to kapetan II klase in 1938, on the outbreak of war he was CO of 16. *Aerodromska Ceta* (airfield company) of 32 LG/6 LP at Krusedol airfield. Helebrant enlisted in the ZNDH in June 1941 as a satnik, and transferred to the HZL in August.

By late October 1942, he had ten confirmed and two unconfirmed (one of which was later upgraded) victories to his credit. Helebrant failed to add to his score during his second tour, and in 1943 he moved to JG 104 and later Fl.Ü.G. He was promoted to nadsatnik and made CO of the HZL's 2/*Kroatien Jagdgruppe* 1 (later renamed 2./JGr *Kro*) in December. Promoted again to bojnik, Helebrant returned to the ZNDH and was appointed CO of 2.ZS in Sarajevo-Rajlovac in August 1944, flying occasional missions. In December he became the first (and last) CO of 1.ZLS, but was posted to ZNDH HQ in early 1945. Helebrant defected to the JA on 20 April, and became deputy CO of *Mostarska Eskadrila*.

Demobilised shortly after war's end, the ace became a clerk in Zagreb and died in 1990. During his combat career Helebrant had survived five forced landings, and claimed three LaGG-3s, two Il-2s, two DB-3s and a single Pe-2, R-5, I-16 and MiG-3 destroyed on the Eastern Front.

Albin Starc (11 kills)

Born on 20 December 1916 in Rijeka, Slovenia, Starc graduated from 1.PS in 1940 and was promoted to porucnik. He had just completed his course at III PS when war broke out.

Joining the ZNDH in April 1941 with the rank of nadporucnik, Starc moved to the HZL in July. He claimed an I-16 in November, and by October 1942 his score had reached nine confirmed and three unconfirmed kills, of which two

This photograph of ppor Albin Starc was taken when he graduated from 1.PS at Pancevo in 1940. Fifty years later, on 18 May 1990, he was presented with the 'Golden Pilot Badge' (*MJV*)

were later upgraded. Starc survived being shot down by Soviet flak, although he was forced to stay in Zagreb through ill health when his unit returned to the Crimea in February 1943.

A pre war communist sympathiser, he defected to Soviet-controlled territory during his 229th combat flight in May 1943. Sent to Krasnodar to train on Yak fighters, Starc returned to Yugoslavia in September 1945 as the pilot of one of 40 Yak-3s which formed 254.LP. The ace remained in the JRV post war, serving mainly in training units, and he retired as a pukovnik during the mid-1970s. It is believed Starc's early war service prevented him from becoming a general. He now lives in Zemun, Yugoslavia.

An official photograph of Tomislav Kauzlaric in the mid 1930s, when he was assigned to 6.LP. Whilst serving as narednik-vodnik I klase with 104.LE, he shot down a Bf 110 on 6 April 1941. Three days after his combat debut, he retreated with the rest of his unit to Bijeljina and thereafter to Sarajevo, where he was captured by *Wehrmacht* troops (*MJV*)

Tomislav Kauzlaric (11 kills)

Born on 21 December 1907 near Delnice, Kauzlaric received his wings from 7.VP in 1932 and duly became a fully fledged military pilot in 1935.

He then trained as a fighter pilot, and after being captured by the Germans in April 1941, Kauzlaric elected to join the ZNDH and then the HZL in July as a stozerni narednik. Promoted to zastavnik, he scored his eleventh, and final, victory in September 1942 and was injured the following month, being sent to Germany for treatment. Kauzlaric rejoined 15.*Staffel* as a newly promoted porucnik in May 1943, but he had not fully recovered from his injuries and was sent back to Croatia.

He resumed flying, with 1.ZJ at Borongaj, in the summer of 1943, and was posted to 21.ZJ in October. Kauzlaric then transferred to the newly

An appreciably older-looking Tomislav 'Toma' Kauzlaric climbs out of Bf 109G 'Black 4' at Armavir airfield in the summer of 1942. The various Croatian pilots that flew this particular *Gustav* claimed at least four Soviet aircraft destroyed (*Authors*)

created 2.ZJ, and he also served as a test pilot during this period, flying a captured Spitfire IX. Badly injured in an accident at Lucko in February 1945, Kauzlaric returned to 2.ZJ as a nadporucnik the following April. On 7 May he flew a Junkers W 34 to northern Italy and surrendered to the Allies. Once released from a PoW camp, Kauzlaric joined his wife and moved to France, where they lived until their return to Yugoslavia in the early 1960s. Settling in Subotica, Kauzlaric died on 31 October 1996.

Vladimir Ferencina and Bf 109E 'Green 15' are seen at Eupatoria in the spring of 1942 (*S Ostric*)

Vladimir Ferencina (10 kills)

Born on 17 October 1905 in Biskupec, Ferencina gained his pilot's wings at 1.VP in Novi Sad in 1934, and became a fighter pilot two years later. Based at Rovine, near Banja Luka, during the April War, he had by then become a kapetan I klase, and CO of 218.BE/69.

Ferencina joined the ZNDH in April 1941 as a satnik, and then transferred to the HZL in July. He subsequently claimed 15(*Kroat*)./ JG 52's first victory the following November. Promoted to bojnik, Ferencina had achieved ten confirmed and four to six unconfirmed victories by August. He became CO of 10.ZLJ in May 1943, and was posted to JG 104 the following July. Appointed deputy CO of the HZL, and later the HZS, Ferencina remained in this position until August 1944, when he returned to ZNDH as deputy CO of 3.ZL, based in Mostar-Jasenica. He was appointed CO of 2.ZS in the autumn, and by war's end the unit had dispersed to airfields near Zagreb. Ferencina and most of his pilots then flew to partisan-held territory, where he was arrested. Freed from prison when Yugoslavia broke ties with the Soviet Union in 1948, he went to live in Zagreb, where he died in the late 1980s.

Major Vladimir Ferencina smiles for the camera at Taman on 23 April 1943. He flew 16 sorties during this month on the Eastern Front, but failed to add to his score. Increased staff duties soon caused him to stop combat flying (*S Ostric*)

Zdenko Avdic (10 kills)

Born on 13 August 1922 in Omis, Avdic was accepted for pilot training during the summer of 1941, and graduated from 1.DPJ, A/B 123 and JG 104 as a fighter pilot in October 1943. Posted to the Crimea as a vodnik, he scored his first kill in November. Avdic claimed a LaGG-3 as his tenth victory during only his 18th combat mission later that month, but was severely wounded during the same sortie, losing his left arm. Evacuated to a military hospital in Odessa, Avdic was transferred a month later to a Luftwaffe recuperation centre in Germany.

Now with an artificial limb, he returned to Zagreb in April 1944 and was posted to ZNDH HQ. By July Avdic had advanced three ranks to castnicki namjesnik, and in May 1945 he graduated from an officers' course but was captured and sent to a PoW camp. Released and then re-arrested, Avdic spent the next 18 months in prison. He later went to work as a clerk in a Zagreb company, becoming its general manager prior to his retirement in 1982. Avdic still lives in Zagreb today. He claimed four LaGG-3s, two P-39s, two La-5s and a single Il-2M3, Yak-1 and A-20.

Bozidar M Bartulovic (8 kills)

Born on 25 May 1923 in Belgrade, Bartulovic lived in Zemun prior to attending 2.PS in Kraljevo. He graduated on 1 April 1941 with the rank of podnarednik.

Joining the ZNDH in May as a vodnik, Bartulovic completed his training as a fighter pilot in November, having attended A/B 120 and JFS 4. Posted to 15(*Kroat*)./JG 52 shortly before the end of the *Staffel*'s first combat tour, he saw no action. Upon returning to the fighting on the Eastern Front in the spring of 1943, Bartulovic claimed eight LaGG-3s in less than 20 months.

Promoted to narednik on 10 April, he then spent time with both JG 104 and Fl.Ü.G, before being posted to 2/*Kro* JGr 1 in December. Bartulovic remained with this unit until July 1944, and flying C.202s and C.205s, he achieved one unconfirmed victory over a B-24. On returning to the ZNDH, he was sent to 2.LJ at Borongaj, where he flew Fi 167s until he was shot down by RAF Mustangs near Sisak on 10 October – he bailed out seriously wounded, a 0.50-cal bullet having shattered his skull and shot away his right eye.

Following a long recovery in Zagreb, Bartulovic was sent on an officers' course. Captured on graduation, and confined in a PoW camp until his release in early 1946, he was subsequently re-arrested and sentenced to 15 years in prison. Freed in 1954, Bartulovic completed engineering studies and lived in Skoplje until 1970, when he emigrated to Germany. He died in Münich on 15 October 1985.

Josip Kranjc (9 kills)

Born on 22 January 1922 in Bjelovar, Slovenia, Kranjc was accepted for pilot training in the summer of 1941 and attended 1.DPJ, A/B 123 and JG 104. Promoted to vodnik in March 1943, and receiving his pilot's wings that same month, Kranjc arrived in the Crimean peninsula in October 1943. He scored his first kill several weeks later, and quickly followed this up with eight more. Kranjc was killed in a flying accident near Perekop on 21 December 1943.

Jure Lasta (8 kills)

Born on 27 January 1915 in Cim, near Mostar, Lasta qualified as an aviation mechanic in 1939, and then graduated from 2.PS, in Kraljevo, later that same year. He attended III PS at Nis, and became a fighter pilot in November 1940. Lasta joined the ZNDH with the rank of vodnik in

This official photograph of Bozidar 'Bosko' Bartulovic as a VVKJ cadet of 2.PS, in Kraljevo, was taken in 1940. For reasons that remain unknown, Bartulovic was imprisoned after the war for longer than any other 15(*Kroat*)./JG 52 pilot, despite his modest rank (*Authors*)

A graduation photo of Jure Lasta, taken after completing the course at 2.PS in 1939. The authors have not been able to discover why he has a porucnik epaulette pinned to his chest, for when this shot was taken, his rank was narednik II klase (*MJV*)

May 1941, moving to the HZL in July and being promoted to narednik. Posted to 15(*Kroat*)./JG 52 at Mariupol in December, Lasta claimed an I-16 in March 1942, but was later admitted to hospital suffering from hepatitis. His illness did not prevent him from being promoted to zastavnik and then porucnik, and he achieved his eighth victory on 28 October 1942. However, during his return flight to base the engine of his Bf 109G exploded and the fighter crashed near Bjelaja river. Lasta did not survive the impact.

Dragutin Gazapi (7 kills)

Born on 2 September 1922 in Kriz, near Zagreb, Gazapi was accepted for pilot training in 1941 and duly attended 1.DPJ, A/B 123 and JG 104. He received his pilot's wings and promotion to narednik in March 1943, and graduated as a fighter pilot the following October.

Gazapi duly claimed his first victory later that month, although he was in turn shot down by several Soviet P-39s in November. Emerging unharmed from this incident, he was killed during his next engagement with communist Airacobras on 27 November. Gazapi's score had reached seven confirmed victories and one unconfirmed by the time of his premature death.

Dragutin Gazapi is seen while a cadet with 1.DPJ, in Borongaj, in late 1941. He claimed seven confirmed victories and one unconfirmed victory in less than a month, but did not survive for long, falling victim to Soviet fighters on 27 November 1943 (*J Novak*)

Left
Safet Boskic and Jure Lasta chat in front of Bf 109E-3 'Green 15' at Mariupol in May 1942. A close inspection of the *Emil's* lower propeller blade reveals the scars from the aircraft's most recent combat (*HPM*)

Vladimir Kres (6 kills)

Born on 10 November 1921 in Zagreb as Vladimir Nahod, the future ace was orphaned within a year of his birth and eventually changed his name to Kres in 1944. After acceptance for pilot training, he attended 1.DPJ, A/B 123 and JG 104. Kres graduated as a pilot and was promoted to vodnik in March 1943, whereupon he was posted to 15(*Kroat*)./JG 52 during its third tour. By March 1944 he had achieved five confirmed and three unconfirmed (one of which was later upgraded) victories, by which time he was the unit's sole combat-ready pilot. Promoted to narednik in May 1944, Kres returned to Croatia in February 1945 and joined 2.ZJ at Lucko. He was a passenger in one of two Junkers W 34s that were flown to Italy in early May to surrender to the Allies. Later returning to Yugoslavia, Kres worked for a film company helping in the production of flying sequences for war films. He currently lives in Zagreb.

Stjepan Radic (5 kills)

Born on 8 April 1920 in Sinj, Radic attended III PS shortly before the outbreak of war, receiving the rank of podnarednik. Joining the ZNDH in May 1941, he transferred to the HZL in July as a vodnik. Posted to 15(*Kroat*)./JG 52 at Mariupol in December 1941, Radic claimed his first victory the following March. Promoted to narednik, he scored his fifth, and last, confirmed kill (an Il-2 near Tuapse) on 29 August 1942, but was in turn hit by flak. Radic crashed into trees while attempting a force-landing, causing his Bf 109 to burst into flames. He had no chance of escape.

Aces high! Kauzlaric, Galic, Radic, Culinovic, Ferencina and Boskic stage a flight briefing for the benefit of the photographer prior to flying a mission in May 1942. At the time of his death on 29 August 1942, Stjepan Radic was the youngest pilot serving with 15(*Kroat*)./JG 52 (*HPM*)

APPENDICES

APPENDIX A

ZNDH/HZL pilots who scored aerial victories during World War 2

Rank	Name	Nationality	VVKJ & RAF	East confirmed	East unconfirmed	NDH confirmed	NDH unconfirmed
sat	Mato Dukovac	Croat		44	1		
sat	Cvitan Galic	Croat		38	5		
puk	Franjo Dzal	Croat		16	3 to 5		
sat	Ljudevit Bencetic	Croat		15	2	1	
npr	Safet Boskic	Bosnian		13	3		
boj	Zlatko Stipcic	Croat	1	12	2		
boj	Mato Culinovic	Croat		12	6		
st nar	Veca Mikovic	Croat		12	2		
st nar	Eduard Martinko	Czech		12	1		
boj	Josip Helebrant	Croat		11	1		
npr	Albin Starc	Slovene		11	1		
zast	Stjepan Martinasevic	Croat		11			
npr	Tomislav Kauzlaric	Croat	1	10			
boj	Vladimir Ferencina	Croat		10	4 to 6		
cas nam	Zdenko Avdic	Croat		10			
nar	Bozidar Bartulovic	Croat		8		1	1
vod	Josip Kranjc	Slovene		9			
por	Jure Lasta	Croat		8			
vod	Dragutin Gazapi	Croat		7	1		
nar	Vladimir Kres	Croat		6	2		
nar	Stjepan Radic	Croat		5	3		
nar	Ivan Baltic	Croat		4	1		
vod	Albin Sval	Slovene		3	2		
st nar	Viktor Mihelcic	Slovene		2			
npr	Nikola Vucina	Croat		2			
vod	Ivan Kulic	Croat				1	2
vod	Asim Korhut	Bosnian				1	1
vod	Jakob Petrovic	Croat				1	1
vod	Leopold Hrastovcan	Croat				1	1
vod	Vladimir Sandtner	Slovak		1	1		
nar	Josip Jelacic	Croat		1	1		
npr	Dragutin Rubcic	Croat	1				
npr	Eduard Banfic	Slovene	1				
sat	Janko Dobnikar	Slovene	2				
sat	Nikola Cvikic	Serb		1			
sat	Vilim Acinger	German		1			
npr	Ivan Jergovic	Croat		1			
por	Zivko Dzal	Croat		1			
por	Mihajlo Jelak	Croat					1
nar	Jeronim Jankovin	Croat		1			
vod	Vladimir Salamon	Croat		1			
vod	Josip Cekovic	Croat					1
ppor	Sime Fabijanovic	Croat	$1/4$				
zast	Mirko Kovacic	Slovene	$1/4$				
zast	Mehmedalija Loxic	Bosnian	$1/4$				

Note for Appendix A

Some uncertainty surrounds the claims of 15(*Kroat*)./JG 52. Many kill claims remained unconfirmed, while others were only confirmed after a long period. There were also many different claim qualifications – confirmed, unconfirmed, allowed, disallowed, probable, possible, witnessed, unwitnessed. Another difficulty in assessing the unit's success is the conflict between Luftwaffe and ZNDH records, which led to so much post war confusion that even today some pilots' scores remain uncertain. For example, an official ZNDH document confirming Mato Dukovac's score to be 44 kills was found recently at the *Vojno-istorijski institut* (Military Archive) in Belgrade, but it is not known whether the RLM credited him with the same score. It should also be noted that HZL pilots were no better at aircraft recognition than many others. This probably explains the disproportionate number of LaGG-3s to Yaks amongst the claims when both types were in Soviet service in equal numbers. Similarly, claims for MiG-3s were made at times, and in particular theatres, when such aircraft were not employed.

APPENDIX B

Comparison of ranks, and their abbrevations

Vazduhoplovstvo Vojske Kraljevine Jugoslavije	VVKJ	Zrakoplovstvo Nezavisne	ZNDH Drzave Hrvatske	Luftwaffe
pukovnik	puk	pukovnik	puk	Oberst
potpukovnik	ppuk	podpukovnik	ppuk	Oberstleutnant
major	maj	bojnik	boj	Major
kapetan I klase	k Ik	nadsatnik	nsat	-
kapetan II klase	k IIk	satnik	sat	Hauptmann
porucnik	por	nadporucnik	npor	Oberleutnant
potporucnik	ppor	porucnik	por	Leutnant
naredник-vodnik I klase	nv Ik	zastavnik	zast	Oberfahnrich
naredник-vodnik II klase	nv IIk	castnicki namjestnik	cas nam	Stabsfeldwebel
naredник-vodnik III klase	nv IIIk	stozerni narednik	st nar	Oberfeldwebel
narednik I klase	nar Ik	narednik	-	Feldwebel
narednik II klase	nar IIk	-	-	Unterfeldwebel
podnarednik I klase	pn Ik	vodnik	vod	Unteroffizier
podnarednik II klase	pn IIk	-	-	Stabsgefreiter
kaplar	kap	razvodnik	razv	Obergefreiter
-	-	desetnik	des	Gefreiter

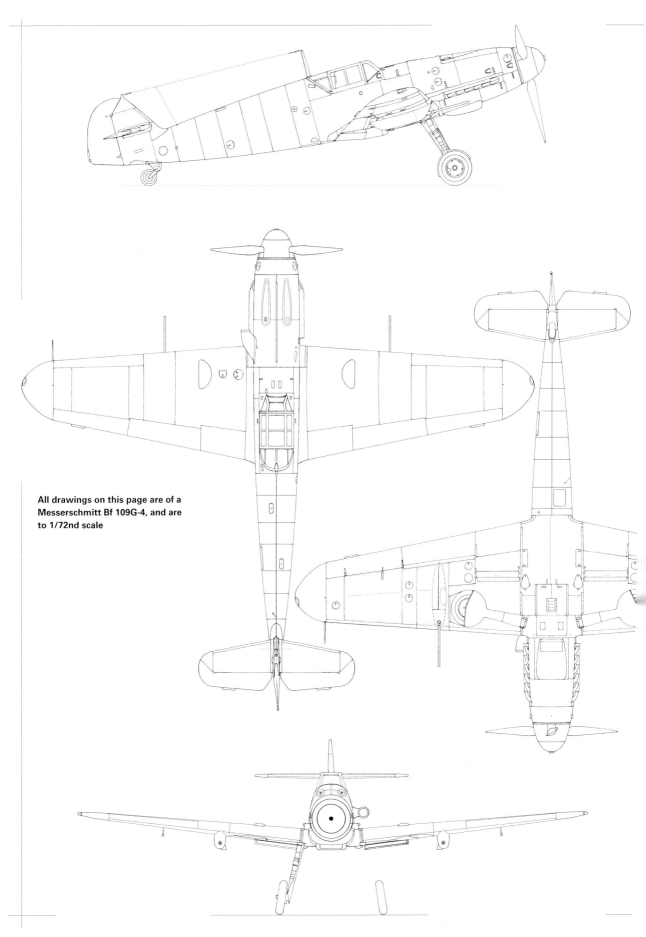

All drawings on this page are of a
Messerschmitt Bf 109G-4, and are
to 1/72nd scale

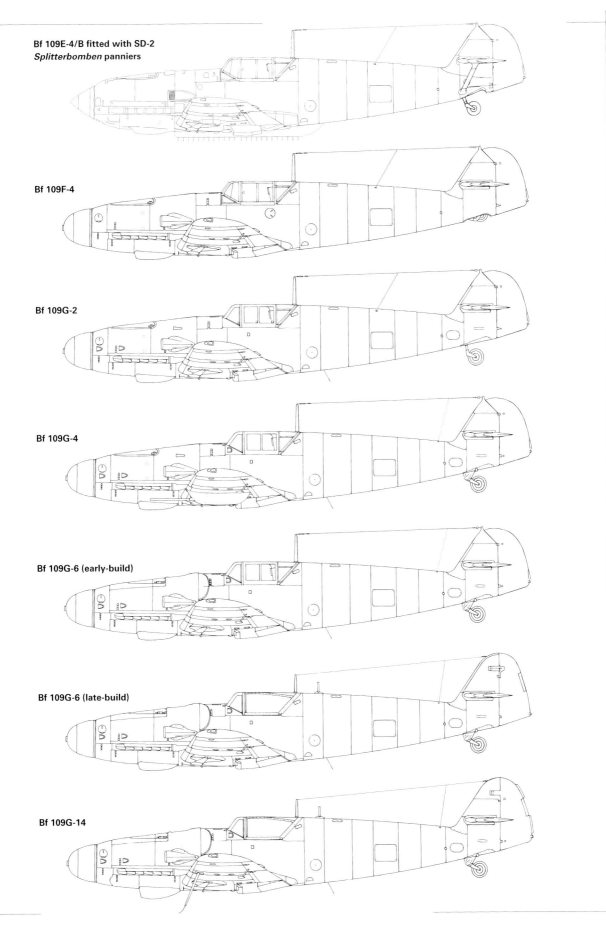

Bf 109E-4/B fitted with SD-2
Splitterbomben panniers

Bf 109F-4

Bf 109G-2

Bf 109G-4

Bf 109G-6 (early-build)

Bf 109G-6 (late-build)

Bf 109G-14

General Note

Very few, if any, HZL and ZNDH pilots had the luxury of their own personal aircraft. Indeed, when veterans were asked, all stressed that each pilot flew whatever fighter was available at the time. The following conclusions as to which pilots were frequent users of which particular aircraft have been drawn from the units' diaries, pilots' log-books, photographs and memoirs.

1

Bf 109E-3a VVKJ Ev.br.(s/n) 2563 'Black L-65' of nv IIIk Cvitan Galic, 103.LE, Veliki Radinci, September 1940

The VVKJ received 'L-65' in March 1940. It wore RLM 65/70 camouflage, which was standard for all VVKJ *Emils*. For reasons unknown, the air intakes on all Yugoslav Bf 109Es remained unpainted. Galic flew 'Black L-65' during manoeuvres at Veliki Radinci airfield in September 1940, and soon afterwards it was transferred to III PS.

2

Bf 109E-3a VVKJ Ev.br.(s/n) 2502 'Black L-2' of k lk Zlatko Stipcic, III PS, Kosor, April 1941

The second of 83 *Emils* aircraft received from Germany, this aircraft was flown to Yugoslavia on 14 August 1939 by Hans-Karl Mayer (a future 39-victory ace). It was severely damaged in November 1939, and sent back to Germany for repairs. Upon its return, the fighter was issued to III PS, then based at Nis, on 9 August. Stipcic subsequently flew six sorties in 'Black L-2' during the April war. The fighter had no wing cannons, its sole armament being two 7.9 mm machine guns with only 330 rounds each, due to a shortage of ammunition at Kosor. This aircraft was destroyed on the ground by Italian fighters on 13 April.

3

Bf 109E-7/trop 'Green 2' of Oberfahnrich Tomislav Kauzlaric, 15(*Kroat*)./JG 52, Taganrog, April 1942

This aircraft has an unusual coat of RLM 76 applied, over which unsymmetrical blotches of RLM 74/75 have been added. It also features a 'Croatian winged shield', the special marking carried on most HZL fighters.

4

Bf 109E-7 'Green 23' of Major Vladimir Ferencina, 15(*Kroat*)./JG 52, Taganrog, April 1942

Major Ferencina flew this aircraft during the spring of 1942. It had an unusually high individual aircraft number. Indeed, few 2-series numbers are known to have been applied to HZL *Emils* during this period.

5

Bf 109E-4 'Green 5' of Oberleutnant Albin Starc, 15(*Kroat*)./JG 52, Eupatoria, May 1942

Another unusual camouflage scheme applied to HZL *Emils* was this underside RLM 76 with overall RLM 70 uppersurfaces. These colours were applied to reduce the fighter's over-sea visibility when viewed from above. This

particular Bf 109 boasts a panel of armoured glass affixed to its windscreen. Albin Starc regularly flew this machine during the siege of Sevastopol.

6

Bf 109E-3 'Green 15' of Major Vladimir Ferencina, 15(*Kroat*)./JG 52, Eupatoria, June 1942

Confusingly, 15. *Staffel* had two 'Green 15s' at the same time! The number '15' was the same size on both aircraft, but the *Balkenkreutz* was moved a little way forward on this particular machine. Vladimir Ferencina claimed at least one kill while flying this *Emil* during June 1942.

7

Bf 109E-3 'Green 15' of Oberfeldwebel Veca Mikovic, 15(*Kroat*)./JG 52, Mariupol, June 1942

Eight circles with victory bars above them, indicating Mikovic's claims, were painted in white on the rudder of 15(*Kroat*)./JG 52's second 'Green 15'. Mikovic claimed two MiG-3s while flying this aircraft on 20 June 1942. Among the other pilots who frequently used the machine were aces Galic, Stipcic, Kauzlaric and Lasta.

8

Bf 109E-3 'Green 11' of Major Mato Culinovic, 15(*Kroat*)./JG 52, Mariupol, July 1942

'Green 11' was one of the *Staffel*'s very last operational *Emils*. The veteran fighter remained in service with the unit until Mato Culinovic damaged it on landing at Mariupol in mid- July 1942.

9

Bf 109E-3 'Green 17' of Feldwebel Stjepan Radic, 15(*Kroat*)./JG 52, Mariupol, July 1942

'Ancient' Bf 109E-3 'Green 17' was frequently flown by Stjepan Radic during June and July 1942. Finally, on 5 August, a *Rotte* comprising Helebrant (in 'Green 17') and Starc (in 'Green 10') flew 15(*Kroat*)./JG 52's last recorded combat mission with the *Emil*.

10

Bf 109G-2 'Black 5' of Oberleutnant Ljudevit Bencetic, 15(*Kroat*)./JG 52, Mariupol, July 1942

One of the first of the long-awaited *Gustavs* to be issued to 15. *Staffel*, this aircraft boasts standard RLM 74/75/76 camouflage, as well as the usual RLM 04 Eastern Front theatre markings. The spinner is one-third white and two-thirds black/green. The eight victory bars on the tailfin indicate Ljudevit Bencetic's score at the time.

11

Bf 109G-2 'Black 7' of Major Mato Culinovic, 15(*Kroat*)./ JG 52, Mariupol, July 1942

'Black 7' survived for more than four months with the *Staffel*. During July 1942 it was Culinovic's personal aircraft, and it carried his ten kill markings on its rudder. Following his return to Croatia, the fighter was usually flown by Stjepan

Martinasevic, who claimed at least two confirmed victories while flying it.

12

Bf 109G-2 Wk-Nr 13463 'Black 8' of Hauptmann Josip Helebrant, 15(*Kroat*)./JG 52, Mariupol, July 1942

Althrough at least eight pilots used this long-lived fighter, Josip Helebrant considered 'Black 8' to be 'his' personal *Gustav*. Strengthening his claim, the ace scored seven confirmed victories and one unconfirmed kill while flying it. The fighter presently boasts just one victory bar on the rudder, but by November ten more would be added.

13

Bf 109G-2/R6 Wk-Nr 13520 'Black 9' of Oberfeldwebel Stjepan Martinasevic, 15(*Kroat*)./JG 52, Armavir, August 1942

Martinasevic claimed two *Chaikas* on 13 August 1942 with 'Black 9'. Sixteen days later, 22-year-old ace Feldwebel Stjepan Radic lost his life when this aircraft crashed near Tuapse after being hit by Soviet flak. Just minutes earlier he had claimed a *Stormovik* for his fifth, and last, victory.

14

Bf 109G-2 Wk-Nr 13438 'Black 10' of Oberfahnrich Safet Boskic, 15(*Kroat*)./JG 52, Kertch, August 1942

Boskic claimed a MiG-3 on 16 August while flying this aircraft. Five days later it received '50 per cent damage' when it crash-landed with Vladimir Ferencina at the controls. The fighter was also used by aces Culinovic, Starc, Helebrant, Stipcic and Kauzlaric, among others.

15

Bf 109G-2/R6 Wk-Nr 13517 'Black 11' of Major Vladimir Ferencina, 15(*Kroat*)./JG 52, Jelisavetinskaya, August 1942

In Vladimir Ferencina's second crash in 11 days, he wrote off this *Kanonenboot* whilst attempting to take off from Jelisaventinskaya on 27 August 1942. Overall damage to the aircraft was estimated at '65 per cent'. A recent arrival with 15(*Kroat*)./JG 52, Wk-Nr 13517 was destroyed before the application of its detailed 'Croatian winged shield' marking could be completed.

16

Bf 109G-2 Wk-Nr 13577 'Black 1' of Oberstleutnant Franjo Dzal, CO of 15(*Kroat*)./JG 52, Jelisavetinskaya, September 1942

After losing his first *Gustav* on 28 July, Franjo Dzal went personally to the depot at Uman on 4 August and collected this particular aircraft. Unfortunately for Dzal, Ferencina sortied in it on 26 August and 'Black 1' was duly hit by flak. The ace was forced to crash-land the fighter in the steppe near Krimskaya, and the *Gustav* duly suffered '30 per cent damage'.

17

Bf 109G-2 Wk-Nr 13432 'Black 3' of Oberfahnrich Cvitan Galic, 15(*Kroat*)./JG 52, Maikop, September 1942

Cvitan Galic used this fighter to down at least seven Soviet aircraft and Ljudevit Bencetic claimed one. Adorning its

rudder were at least 17 white circles outlined in black and topped with bars containing red stars, each one indicating a Galic kill.

18

Bf 109G-2 'Black 4' of Leutnant Jure Lasta, 15(*Kroat*)./JG 52, Jelisavetinskaya, October 1942

This aircraft was flown by no less than 11 different pilots during its time on the Eastern Front. On 9 September 1942, Martinasevic claimed a DB-3, on 1 October Lasta (who flew 'Black 4' most of all) destroyed a MiG-3 and on 25 October Starc downed two LaGGs, all while flying this aircraft.

19

Bf 109G-2 Wk-Nr 13577 'Black double-chevron 1' of Oberstleutnant Franjo Dzal, CO of 15(*Kroat*)./JG 52, Maikop, October 1942

This is the same aircraft as featured in profile 16 ('Black 1'), although by this stage in its career its camouflage scheme has been changed – perhaps it was resprayed whilst under repair? The wing and fuselage crosses have been painted black and a double-chevron added to both sides of the fuselage. Dzal claimed seven kills and Ferencina one whilst flying this aircraft. A long-lived *Gustav*, Wk-Nr 13577 was later passed on to II./JG 52 and then sold to Finland in May 1943. Coded MT-225, it became the first Bf 109G to be issued to the Finnish air force's elite fighter unit, HLeLv 24. In turn assigned to 1Lt Lauri Nissinen (32.333 victories), he used it to down the first kill attributed to a Finnish Bf 109 (on 14 April 1944) when he destroyed a German Ju 188 that had entered Finnish airspace without prior notice, and without recognisbale national markings. The veteran fighter was eventually written off by 9.5-kill ace SSgt Viljo Kauppinen when he crash-landed after being wounded in combat with a P-39 from 196.IAP on 7 June 1944. See *Osprey Aviation Elite 4 - Lentolaivue 24* for further details.

20

Bf 109G-2 'Yellow 6' of Leutnant Cvitan Galic, 15(*Kroat*)./JG 52, Kertch IV, May 1943

Cvitan Galic flew this aircraft almost exclusively during his second combat tour, gaining at least eight kills while doing so. The fighter's stylised Croat shield has silver instead of white wings.

21

Bf 109G-2/R6 'Yellow 11' of Oberleutnant Albin Starc, 15(*Kroat*)./JG 52, Gukovo, May 1943

This brand new aircraft ended up in Soviet hands after Albin Starc's defection on 14 May 1943. And having only been on stength with the unit for a mere 48 hours, the 'Croat winged shield' was not applied and the small white '11' remained in front of the *Balkenkreutz*. Test-flown by Soviet ace Boris Yeryomin (23 kills), the aircraft was destroyed a short while later in a take-off accident whilst being flown by another pilot.

22

Bf 109G-2 'Yellow 12' of Oberleutnant Ljudevit Bencetic, 15(*Kroat*)./JG 52, Taman, May 1943

Bencetic claimed his sole confirmed kill in 1943 with this aircraft on 6 May. The fighter's 'Croat winged shield' boasts silver wings, and the black square forward of the *Balkenkreutz* denotes where the small white number 12 (see previous profile) had been located.

23
Bf 109G-4 of Unteroffizier Vladimir Kres, 15(*Kroat*)./JG 52, Karankut, November 1943
Depicted soon after it had arrived on the unit from Germany, no number has yet been assigned to this fighter. The 'Croat winged shield' is still not finished either. Theatre markings consist of an RLM 04 tailband, underside wing-tips and underside engine cowling.

24
Bf 109G-6 'Black chevron 1' of Oberleutnant Mato Dukovac, CO of 15(*Kroat*)./JG 52, Kertch, November 1943
Dukovac used this aircraft until he was shot down in it by a Soviet P-39 on 25 February 1944. At one time its chevron marking had been painted in a lighter colour, probably green.

25
Bf 109G-6 Wk-Nr 18497 'White 13' of Unteroffizier Zdenko Avdic, 15(*Kroat*)./JG 52, Kertch, November 1943
This aircraft features standard camouflage and markings, but no 'Croat' shield. Note that its landing gear covers have been removed. Avdic claimed his last kill, and was then severely wounded, while flying this aircraft on 21 November 1943.

26
Bf 109G-6 'White 5' of Unteroffizier Josip Kranjc, 15(*Kroat*)./JG 52, Karankut, November 1944
Kranjc flew this aeroplane on several occasions. It wore standard camouflage and markings, with a wide white spiral on the spinner. The fighter's landing gear covers were removed in line with common practice on muddy airfields in the Soviet Union.

27
Bf 109G-6 Wk-Nr 19680 'Red 9' of Unteroffizier Eduard Martinko, 15(*Kroat*)./JG 52, Kertch, November 1943
Martinko crash-landed this aircraft on 12 November 1943 after being mistakenly hit by German flak. Its red number had a black outline, and traces of the former radio-code 'MD' could be seen beneath the '9'.

28
G.50bis '3504' of por Tomislav Kauzlaric, 21.Lovacko Jato, Borongaj, April 1944
One of several Fiats flown by Kauzlaric on anti-partisan sorties, this aircraft was the fourth of its type received by the unit from an initial batch of ten in June 1942. It features standard Italian two-tone camouflage, namely *Grigio Azzuro Chiaro* 1 undersides and *Verde Oliva Scuro* 2 uppersurfaces. Underside wing-tips, tail band and numbers have been applied in *Giallo Chromo 7*. On 3 June 1944 an order for the removal of the yellow fuselage bands was issued, and they were subsequently overpainted with dark grey.

29
C.202 'Black 1' of Hauptmann Josip Helebrant, CO of 2/JGr *Kro*, Pleso, May 1944

'Black 1' was one of the aircraft received from *Luftpark Nis*, and they differed from other Macchis issued to the Croats through the application of an RLM 04 yellow tail band and lower engine cowling panel. The fighter wore Luftwaffe markings applied to standard *Regia Aeronautica* camouflage – *Grigio Azzuro Chiaro* on the underside and *Sabbia* uppersurfaces, covered with stains of *Verde Oliva Squoro* and *Nocciola Chiaro*.

30
MS 406c '2323' of sat Ljudevit Bencetic, CO of 14.ZJ, Zaluzani, September 1944
This aircraft has RLM 65 undersides and RLM 02/71 uppersurfaces. Luftwaffe codes and the fuselage *Balkenkreutz* have been overpainted with RLM 02, while the rest of the fuselage is covered with RLM 02/71 blotches on an RLM 65 base. The tail fin is in RLM 71. Bencetic flew one sortie in '2323' on 19 September 1944 in an effort to stop a NOVJ attack on Banja Luka. The aircraft was one of three operational Moranes captured at Zaluzani, and later incorporated into *Eskadrila 5. Korpusa*.

31
Bf 109G-10 'Black 4' (2104) of Boj Zlatko Stipcic, 2.LJ, Lucko, March 1945
The aircraft wears new ZNDH markings and RLM 76/81/83 camouflage. The rudder, fuselage and cowling bands, 'V' identification marking on the underside of the left wing, underside wing-tips and 2.LJ emblem beneath the cockpit were painted in RLM 04. Stipcic flew this late-build *Gustav* on at least two sorties during March 1945, and on 16 April nar Sandtner used it to defect to Falconara, in Italy.

32
Yak-3 'Yellow 12' of kap Miljenko Lipovscak, CO of 113. Lovacki Puk, Pleso, May 1945
A former ZNDH pilot, kap Lipovscak flew several sorties with this aircraft during the closing stages of the war. Before being transferred to the JRV, this colourful Yak was flown by ppol Sergei S Shchirov, leading ace of 267.IAP. The markings on the engine cowling denote his decorations, the white stars his 21 victories (one of them being Josip Helebrant's Bf 109, claimed whilst flying a Yak-1 on 6 October 1942), and behind the cockpit, on both sides of the fuselage, is a caricature of a white eagle grabbing a 'rabbit-like' Joseph Goebbels. The Yakovlev fighter is depicted in its post war colours after the Soviet stars had been over-painted and full JRV markings applied.

Back cover
Bf 109G-10 'Black 3' (2103) of maj Josip Helebrant, *Mostarska Eskadrila*, Jasenice, May 1945
Nar Tatarevic defected to the JA in this aircraft on 20 April 1945, and it immediately received new markings – red stars over 'Zvonimir' crosses on the wings, a Yugoslav three-colour scheme on the tail and large red stars on the dark green over-painted fuselage 'Zvonimir crosses. Josip Helebrant flew the fighter on three combat-sorties against the *Chetniks* in Bosnia between 7 and 9 May. On the last occasion, he force-landed after losing his way in deteriorating weather, inflicting serious damage on the *Gustav*.

BIBLIOGRAPHY

Ajdic, G, and Jerin, Z, *Letalstvo in Slovenci od prve do druge svetovne vojne, II.* Ljubljana, 1990

Amico, F, and Valentini, G, *The Messerschmitt 109 in Italian Service 1943-45.* USA, 1985

Bernad, D, *Rumanian Air Force 1938-1947.* USA, 1999

Bernad, D et al, *Horrido - Legicsatak a keleti fronton.* Budapest, 1992

Cull, Brian *249 at War.* London,1997

Cull, Brian et al, *Wings over Suez.* London, 1996

Cumichrast, P, and Klabnik, V, *Slovenske letectvo 1939–1944 (part II).* Slovakia, 2000

Dimitrijevic, B, *April 1941.* Belgrade, 2001

Feoktisov, S I, *V nebe Tuapse.* Russia, 1995

Frka, D et al, *Zrakoplovstvo Nezavisne Drzave Hrvatske 1941–1945.* Zagreb, 1998

Green, William, *Warplanes of the Third Reich.* London, 1979

Keskinen, K et al, *Messerschmitt Bf 109G.* Finland, 1991

Kljakic, D, *Oni su branili Beograd.* Zagreb, 1980

Kolo, A, and Dimitrijevic, B, *Spitfajer.* Belgrade, 1997

Komanda, RV and PVO, *Cuvari naseg neba.* Belgrade, 1977

Kostic, B, *Plamen nad Beogradom.* Belgrade, 1991

Likso, T, *Hrvatsko Ratno Zrakoplovstvo u Drugome Svjetskome Ratu.* Croatia, 1998

Likso, T, *Letacka karijera Miljenka Lipovscaka 1939–1980.* Croatia, 2000

Mikic, V, *Nemacka avijacija u Jugoslaviji 1941–1945.* Belgrade, 1999

Mikic, V, *Zrakoplovstvo Nezavisne Draeave Hrvatske 1941–1945.* Belgrade, 2000

Pejcic, P, *Prva i Druga Eskadrila NOVJ.* Belgrade, 1991

Price, Dr Alfred, *Luftwaffe Handbook 1939–1945.* London, 1986

Prien, Jochen, and Rodeike, Peter, *Messerschmitt Bf 109 F, G, K.* USA, 1995

Olynyk, F, *USAAF (Mediterranean Theater) Credits for*

Destruction of Enemy Aircraft in Air-to-Air Combat World War II. USA, 1987

Otovic, D, and Nikic, J. *Vazdusne bitke za ranjenike.* Belgrade, 1986

Rajlich, J, and Sehnal, J, *Slovak Airmen 1939–1945.* Czechoslovakia, 1991

Ries, K, *Deutsche Flugzeugführerschulen und ihre Maschinen 1919–1945.* Stuttgart, 1988

Rosch, B C, *Luftwaffe Codes, Markings and Units 1939–1945.* USA, 1995

Shores, Christopher, *Luftwaffe Fighter Units – Mediterranean 1941-1945.* London, 1978

Shores, Christopher, *Luftwaffe Fighter Units —Russia 1941–1945.* London 1978

Shores, Christopher, *Luftwaffe Fighter Units – Europe 1942–1945. London,* 1979

Shores, Christopher at al, *Air war for Yugoslavia, Greece and Crete.* London, 1987

Vigna, A, *Aeronautica Italiana — Dieci anni di storia 1945–1952.* Italy, 1999

Vojnoistorijski Institut, *Zbornik dokumenata i podataka o NOR Jugoslovenskih naroda (volume II).* Belgrade, 1967

Weal, E C, *Combat Aircraft of World War Two.* London, 1977 *Zavrsne operacije za oslobodjenje Jugoslavije (book 9).* Belgrade, 1986

MAGAZINES AND PERIODICALS
(VARIOUS ISSUES)

Aerei
Aeroplan
Aero magazin
Air Pictorial
Avions
Der Adler
Front
Historie a plastikove modelarstvi
Hrvatska krila
Hrvatski vojnik
Insignia
JP 4 - Mensile di Aeronautica
Let
Luftwaffe Süd-Ost
Plastic kits revue
Revi
Vjesnik oruznih snaga

INDEX

References in **bold** refer to illustrations (commentary locators in brackets)